Ambassador Ton,
All the legal rights of the
Kingdom of God are yours Now!

"Fraud"

What God Has to Say About
the Tactics of the Enemy.

By G.A. Repple

D1372203

1

The Repple Minute
101 Normandy Road
Casselberry FL 32707
Tel | 407.339.9090
TheReppleMinute.com

ISBN: 978-1-7916-8087-9

What others are saying about "Fraud"

"These writings have filled a hunger for non-fundamentalist truth and freedom in living that I have yearned to know for years. I cannot thank you enough and love you enough for pouring out your heart. I could not have discovered these truths on my own. They were not really a part of my own upbringing or spiritual formation. It took your choice to follow God and relate all this and our close friendship, mentoring, for me to wake up and perhaps experience these truths for the first time in my own life. For the past two years, I have had a more powerful and influential ministry, because I have chosen to test, believe, and now closely follow what you have related to me in your daily writings. I have experienced a spiritual maturing I was not at all expecting to discover.

For all readers of this book: Buy a case of these books for any leadership group you influence. Consider spending time as a group pulling out and talking together about the meaningful promises in brother Glenn's writings."

Dr. Scott Preissler, Ph.D, M.Ed., M.S., M.A.
Executive Director
The National Center for Stewardship & Generosity

State Missionary for Stewardship
The Georgia Baptist Convention
Duluth, Georgia

"Over the course of my faith journey for the past ten years, Glenn Repple has served as a confidant, teacher, and friend. Most of all he has modeled for me not just in his words, but through his actions, what it means to steward the King of Kings' resources and wealth. As business and ministry leaders we are called by God to serve as Kings/Priests in the marketplace. Unfortunately, many of us (me included) have been willing to settle for less by accepting the "Fraud" that was committed against us by the enemy of our souls. Our very identity was stolen and we accepted life as 'slaves to sin.' The time has come for each of us to cast aside the lies and deceit the Gates of Hades has thrust upon this generation and break free to a deeper understanding of our true identity as sons and daughters of the Living God, our Father in Heaven. For such a time as this, it is up to us to answer the Call of God to take up this challenge to overcome darkness and evil with good, as men and women of courage doing battle in the heavenlies for the bodies and souls of men and women (Rev 18). Read this book "Fraud" and you will be equipped to join us as fellow sons and daughters of the King of Kings on this final quest to see the Kingdom of God manifest in our generation, in the here and now, in and through the marketplace. The time has come to reclaim not only our identity; but our very lives, families, communities and nations."

Tom Stansbury

"FRAUD....like all things in the Kingdom has so many different forms and levels of charges to be made against the one that lies, cheats and steals from mankind daily. This is an excellent place for young believers to turn to solidify truth in their walks with GOD. It is the Bible made relevant for Believers at any level of maturity in the LORD...The value though of making things simple and clear, is that too many believers that have served GOD for decades are still young in the LORD maturity wise.

There are plenty of Authors with too many degrees that love to make the Word deep and typically drawing all men unto themselves while Brother Repple has a truly pure objective here. His heart for the lost bleeds through the words put in his heart to share. Perhaps I have a bias having started to get to know this kingdom general personally...but only a few pages into this work of love, I had seen his teaching gift come to life in print.

Honored....never thought one could enjoy FRAUD to this degree. "

Donald Ward.

Trusted Adviser
Golden Connector-Author-Speaker-Master Mentor
State Director of CEOCLUBS FLORIDA
Radio Podcast Host to "Resurrecting YOUR Dreams"
Executive Producer - Fishers of Men Entertainment Group
Reality TV Show Host ABOVE C LEVEL

"My friend Glenn Repple's book needed to be written. I was fortunate enough to part of Glenn's friends to receive each day the next reading of the 48 "Fraud" Days and amazingly each one was exactly what I needed in my life at that moment. Read a "Fraud" Day each day and you can't help but reflect on it and feel the power of God's love. I guarantee you will want to share this book with your friends."

Tom Mears
Author of "Serve With Love"
Chairman of Burgerville LLC

"Glenn Repple has done an outstanding job of explaining God's simple and profound truths while exposing the enemy and how he steals our identity of those truths through lies and fraud. For every truth in God's word the devil (or man) speaks lies to counter those truths. Glen explains this without planting a fear of a devil under every rock. Well done Glenn. Great work and great read!"

Ford Taylor
Founder
The FSH Group/ TL Transformational Leadership
Author: "Relational Leadership"

"As one reads these teachings, the reality and power of God comes through to your spirit in new and refreshing ways. Your identity, purpose, and destiny are illustrated by the Spirit of God living in you. To God be the Glory."

Max W. Hooper , Ph.D, D.Min., Ph.D., Th.D , D.Min.
Follower of Jesus

"Experts in currency train individuals to recognize counterfeit by simply using real money. When you know what's real, you can then spot what's not. As you live out your faith authentically in a fraudulent world will those you touch discover you're the real deal? By including *'Fraud'* in your daily devotions, it will heighten any counterfeit areas in your life so you will be authentic, just as Jesus intended."

Dr. George Cope
Vision Orlando

"After knowing and watching Glenn Repple for 30 years, I can assure you he is "no fraud." Fraud is a book that reminds us that we all have a great Enemy who is seeking to put fraudulent thoughts in our minds and hearts. Glenn has taught me by his life and now this book how to live life in light of my true identity as a child of the King."

Jack McGill
Elevate Orlando

"The only thing worse than fraudulent activity, is when it's undiscovered. Through the history of mankind, Satan has used every tool in his fraudulent tool case to deceive and convince us of every notion that goes against the true Word of God. In his book "Fraud" Glenn Repple does a masterful job of uncovering Satan as a fraud. He also helps us understand the depths of his deception and the lengths he'll go, to impose his will and lies on God's people, which includes; stealing our hope, justice, truth, but more important our identity. Finally, Glenn marches us down the road to victory in Christ Jesus, despite the enemies attempts to derail us. "Fraud" is an awesome work of God, by an awesome man of God."

Dexter D. Sanders
Leader of the Back 2 Movement

"Glenn Repple has been my spiritual mentor and encourager for 23 years. We have been walking the path of transformation together with the Holy Spirit. It is been exciting to see and be a part of the manifestation of Christ in Glenn by the presence of the Holy Spirit. This book is the culmination of the transformation that has taken place in Glenn so far and expresses his deep and growing relationship with Father, Son and Spirit. Glenn is truly a man after God's own heart and I can't wait to see and be a part of his continued journey as the Spirit leads us."

W. Bruce Woodard, EA
BSi Consulting Services, Inc.
Altamonte Springs, FL 32701

"This is Glenn Repple at his best as he pours out his heart in this inspiring book. It is definitely a great beginning and my hope is that Glenn will be inspired to write a number of follow-ups that get progressively deeper volume by volume. I am honored to call Glenn my friend and genuine Christian brother."

Art Ally, President
Timothy Plan Family of Biblically Responsible Mutual Funds

"John 8:32 tells us that "we should know the truth and the truth will set us free". Many of us not only do not know the truth but are not free. Glenn Repple in his latest book "Fraud" helps us to know the truth so we may walk in our freedom in Christ. A must reed for those who desire to be free from the lies and attacks of the enemy."

Patrice Tsague
Chief Servant Officer
Nehemiah Project International Ministries

FOREWORD

I am writing this book that you will experience God's Glory.

God's Glory is:

HIS PRESENCE,
HIS POWER and
HIS GOODNESS.
HIS AGAPE[1] LOVE.

I am writing this book that you will know that:

God is real.
Jesus Christ the Anointed One is real.
the Holy Spirit is real.
I am writing this book that you will better understand the three major historical events which are:

Creation
Fall
Redemption

---

[1] (*) AGAPE LOVE is God the Father's, God the Son's and the Holy Spirits divine Love. It is steadfast, unconditional and unselfish. You can't earn it, it is given out of AGAPE LOVE. It is the very character of our triune God. It is unlike man's human love which is fickle, conditional and selfish.

I am writing this book that the Holy Spirit will reveal your true identity.

Who are you?

- You are the Righteousness of God in Christ Jesus
- You are a child of God in the family of God, with a Father who loves you unconditionally and has known you before the earth was formed and shaped you in your mother's womb.
- You are an heir of God and a joint-heir with Jesus Christ.

I am writing this book that you will believe, know and understand God's AGAPE love in sending Jesus to earth:

1. Who redeemed and restored mankind back to God's image, likeness and original value in fellowship, sonship, purpose, righteousness and destiny in Christ Jesus.

2. Who redeemed, restored, liberated and freed mankind from the satanic rule of this world of fear, sickness, shame, guilt, condemnation, death, sin, lack, scarcity, unforgiveness, bitterness, hate and injustice by reclaiming back God's original plan for man to have Authority and Power so that we can have Dominion over all creation in the Justice of God in Christ Jesus to those who are Born Again.

3. Who redeemed and restored LIFE, SHALOM PEACE and REST now in Christ Jesus by forgiving ALL sin, removing ALL sin and forgetting ALL sin.

I write this book that you will:

- grow in the AGAPE love and understanding of the resurrected Christ
- The Word of God will be revealed to you through the Holy Spirit
- That your faith in Christ Jesus will grow so that you experience God's Presence, Power and Goodness and AGAPE LOVE daily, moment by moment.

May the Holy Spirit reveal Truth to you as you read and listen to **TheReppleminute.com**.

The Holy Spirit is TRUTH and reveals HIS truth in three ways:

1. By the need for a Savior
2. That the Savior is revealed through the Holy Spirit in your new identity of RIGHTEOUSNESS
3. That the Savior has taken all JUDGEMENT and declared JUSTICE for ALL who believe in HIM.

Glenn A. Repple

Orlando FL

13

Dedication

This book is dedicated to my family my wife Joanie in covenant since 1972. Son Bryan Repple and daughter Kimberly Von Ancken and Erik Von Ancken, grandchildren Sydney Von Ancken and Luke Von Ancken.

Special thanks to all those who have encourage me to put the morning minutes into a book. Thank you.

Special thanks to Erik Von Ancken who has edited many of the morning minutes over a 12 year period along with Holly Rogers. Thank you.

Special thanks to my mother Vera Guthrie Repple and father Karl William Repple.

My mother modeled the grace and love of God. My father taught me to do what is right "Do the right thing". He knew and understand that there are laws to life which make all things work. They both exemplified a generous life.

INTRODUCTION

The Greatest Fraud Ever Committed

Mankind has been ripped off and they don't even know it. People are accepting a life below their God intended purpose and design. This book is a wake up call for you to know your identity, purpose and destiny. You and I have bought into the lies and deceitfulness of the greatest fraud.

Jesus said in John 8:31-32 MKJV, "If you abide in My word, you are My disciples indeed. [32] And you shall know the truth, and the truth shall make you free."

If you are seeking to know your FATHER, the Truth of your identity and the AGAPE Love your Father has for you, then you will want to read this book faithfully to gain understanding of your identity.

My people perish for a lack of knowledge.

Here are three big questions:

1. What are the three greatest events in history?
2. Why is there an increase in pornography, suicide, divorce, fear, social unrest, mass murders, sex trafficking, babies aborted, hate, violence, men wanting to become women and women wanting to become men?
3. Which is greater and more powerful what you see or what you don't see?

Answer to Question 1: The three biggest historical events ever are as follows:

1. **Creation -** God spoke the earth into existence and gave man dominion and reign over all the earth
2. **The Fall -** the satanic rule of earth
3. **Redemption** - mankind returned into right standing with their Father

Answer to Question 2: The fall is the cause for the increase in pornography, suicide, divorce, fear, social unrest, mass murders, sex trafficking, babies aborted, men wanting to become women and women wanting to become men.

Answer to Question 3: Which is greater and more powerful, what you see or what you don't see?

"Faith empowers us to see that the universe was created and beautifully coordinated by the power of God's words! He spoke and the invisible realm gave birth to all that is seen."
- *Hebrews 11:3 TPT*

God spoke creation into existence with words. God's Word is Spirit and Life. The unseen created the seen. The unseen is more powerful than the natural seen world. God is Spirit. He created the natural world for man to have authority, dominion and enjoy HIS creation.

The problem is man's lost identity as sons and daughters of God in the family of God as their Father.

Creation is the first major event in history. God made man in His image and likeness to be His sons and daughters like Him in His family with God as their Father. We were made as eternal Spirit being with Agape Love. He designed us to remain in relationship with Him and that God would be the source of man's Agape Love. God's original design is that the entire world would experience the goodness of God and God's Agape love flowing through His children so that his children would fill and subdue the earth with His image and His Agape love.

But

The Fall is the second greatest event in history. Mankind lost his likeness and closeness as sons and daughters with their Father in the Garden of Eden by Satan's Fraud committed on all mankind through Adam. Man was reduced to living by his own feelings, thoughts and desires. Man lived by what seemed right to him. Man is now living for his own selfishness.

Man attempts to replace the Agape Love of the Father and their identity as a son and daughter which was once enjoyed, with the human love, attention, affirmation, acceptance, esteem, identity through people, possessions and circumstances.

The consequences of the Fall - men and women are born with an orphan spirit looking for their Father's Agape Love. They are born into the dominion of Satan. They are born into to a world of sickness and disease. They are born with a spirit of poverty, rejection and offense filled with fear, lack, insecurity, lack of trust, bitterness, anger, blame, self-effort, self-dependency, self-consciousness, unforgiveness and selfishness. Men and women are born into sickness and disease.

Symptoms of the Fall

Fear holds you in bondage from God's perfect AGAPE love.

Spiritual Death is eternal separation from God. **Guilt** is an internal confession that "I am not forgiven".

Condemnation is an internal confession that "My life is worthy of judgment because of what I have done."

Shame is the internal confession that "This is still who I am. I am a sinner".

Poverty is the internal confess that "I am not good enough".

Sickness and Disease is part of consequence of the curse of the law with a disbelief that God can heal.

Orphan the confession that I am self-made.

Injustice-the confession that, "I will get even".

Hatred and Strife the confession that "it is all about ME".

So, what is the solution from the fall of mankind?

Redemption is the third major historical event in history.
This is God's AGAPE love plan for mankind.

Redemption and Restoration
as a New Creation in Christ Jesus

> "¹⁷ Therefore if any person is [ingrafted] in Christ (the Messiah) he is a new creation (a new creature altogether); the old [previous moral and spiritual condition] has passed away. Behold, the fresh *and* new has come!"
> -   *2 Corinthians 5:17 AMPC*

Mankind was born into the fallen world. God's AGAPE love plan for mankind is redemption from poverty, sickness and spiritual death. God is **Spirit** and God is AGAPE **Love**.

The born-again man is made in the image and likeness of God through the redemptive work of Jesus Christ's blood on the cross.

The fraudster through the fall caused spiritual death, yet God in Christ Jesus has given you new Spiritual Birth. You are alive with the Holy Spirit living in you now.

"For you [who are born-again have been reborn from above—spiritually transformed, renewed, sanctified and] are all children of God [set apart for His purpose with full rights and privileges] through faith in Christ Jesus."
- *Galatians 3:26 AMP*

Jesus came to redeem mankind back to Father God. Jesus redeemed mankind from the curse of the law which is poverty, sickness and spiritual death. Jesus redeemed mankind into right standing with God now. Just like mankind had never sinned. God sees mankind through the blood of Jesus Christ.

God sees mankind as spotless, clean without sin because of the finished work of Jesus Christ on the cross. Jesus Christ restored mankind back to their father's Agape Love. Jesus Christ restored mankind back into the family of God as children of God as sons and daughters of God.

Mankind was made in God's image and likeness which is Spirit and Love - and filled with Agape Love. Man is a Love Being. Man was restored into Agape Love through Jesus Christ so that they could love others and subdue the world with God's Love.

Jesus came to redeem man into a New Creation, Born Again in which the past old nature is gone and the New Nature in Christ Jesus has come alive in love.

Heaven has come to earth to transform man back to the original design and purpose as Spirit Beings made in the image and Likeness of God. Communion and union with God in eternal fellowship is restored.

Consequences of Restoration and Redemption

All guilt, shame, condemnation, and all effects of sin has been cleansed by the blood of Jesus Christ. God sees you through the blood of Jesus Christ as if you have never sinned. You have been made Righteous with right standing with God. God sees you as his son or daughter in His family waiting for you to receive all His Agape Love. His Holy Spirit lives in you now as a transformed New Creation in Christ Jesus.

The Symptom

Is an overflowing Agape Love living in you through the Holy Spirit which brings, rest, perfect Shalom Peace, Soul Salvation and a Joy which is unending.

The three biggest historical events ever are as follows:

1. **Creation** - God spoke the earth into existence and gave man dominion and reign over all the earth
2. **The Fall** - the satanic rule of earth
3. **Redemption** - mankind returned into right standing with their Father

1

Fraud

"Fraud" Day 1

First published September 21, 2018 in the Fraud Series – The Repple Minute

Day 1 of the Fraud committed by Satan against man

Fraud

Wikipedia defines fraud as follows: in law, fraud is the deliberate deception to secure unfair or unlawful gain, or to deprive a victim of a legal right.

Merriam-Webster defines fraud as follows: intentional perversion of truth in order to induce another to part with something of value or to surrender a legal right.

What was the biggest fraud that has ever happened?

_____

When did it happen?

_____

Where did it happen?

_____

Who was involved?

_____

- Your birthright/inheritance has been stolen.
- Your identity has been stolen. You are an orphan.
- Your purpose and destiny have been stolen.

Satan deceived Adam and Eve and fraudulently stole mankind's identity, purpose, destiny, birthright and inheritance. Mankind's identity is in the family of God as a beloved child of God. God gave man dominion and authority to rule and reign over all creation. The Father has an inheritance for HIS CHILDREN in HIS FAMILY. Mankind's destiny is eternal as a Spiritual being made in the image and likeness of God. Man's purpose is to be in communion with God the FATHER, who AGAPE LOVES mankind unconditionally.

Adam and Eve, by believing the fraud,

- exchanged mankind's identity, purpose, destiny, birthright, inheritance, dominion, and authority to rule and reign

for

- spiritual death, sickness, regret, spirit of offense, injustice, anger, bitterness, fear, worry, anxiety, restlessness, blame, unforgiveness, shame, guilt, condemnation and Satan becoming the prince of this world.

Now the Good News!

> "The reason the Son of God was made manifest (visible) was to undo (destroy, loosen, and dissolve) the works the devil [has done]."
> - *1 John 3:8b AMPC*

> "For the Lord is good; His mercy *and* loving-kindness are everlasting, His faithfulness *and* truth endure to all generations."
> - *Psalms 100:5 AMPC*

Jesus Christ redeemed mankind to bring us back into communion with God. Jesus Christ restored mankind back to his original value, purpose and destiny. Jesus died and rose again. HE defeated the works of the fraudulent Satan and brought JUSTICE to all mankind through HIS SHED BLOOD, death and resurrection. Mankind's legal rights have been restored. Mankind has been found not guilty for the frauds committed against God. Mankind can choose to believe and trust in the Resurrected Christ or continue to believe and trust the fraudulent Satan.

I choose Life in Christ with the Holy Spirit living in me.

2

Spirit Being

"Fraud" Day 2

First published September 24, 2018 in the Fraud Series – The Repple Minute

Day 2 of the Fraud committed by Satan against man

Spirit Being

Satan committed fraud in the Garden of Eden by stealing Man's identity as a Spirit Being. Man has a legal and Judicial right to be restored back to the image and likeness of God as a Spirit Being.

> "God is a **Spirit** (a **spirit**ual Being) and those who worship Him must worship Him in **spirit** and in truth (reality)."
> - *John 4:24*

> "It **is the Spirit** who gives **life** [He **is the Life**-giver]; **the** flesh conveys no benefit whatever [**there is** no profit in it]. **The word**s (truths) that I have been speaking to you are **spirit and life**."
> - *John 6:63 AMPC*

God breathed life into the nostrils of man. Life is in the Spirit. God created man in HIS image and likeness as a spirit Being. God restored mankind back to a spirit Being in Christ Jesus.

> "Jesus answered, "I tell you the truth, no one can enter the kingdom of God unless he is born of water and the **Spirit**. Flesh (physical) gives birth to flesh (physical), but the Spirit gives birth to spirit. You should not be surprised at my saying, 'You must be born again (in the Spirit).' The wind blows wherever it pleases. You hear its sound, but you cannot tell where it comes from or where it is going. So it is with everyone born of the Spirit.""
> *- John 3:5-8*

For the born-again believer the **Spirit which resides in you is the same Spirit which raised Jesus from the dead**. It is the same Spirit that God breathed into man who was formed from the dust of the ground. **Real Life is in the Spiritual realm**. The Spirit is the life-giving part of your body. When the spirit leaves, the body dies. **Life is in the Spirit, not in the flesh**.

Your old nature is SUBDUED which seeks to satisfy the flesh (physical); the new born-again nature filled with the Holy Spirit is immersed and washed in the blood of Christ Jesus. Your thinking, emotions, five senses and body is being renewed by God's Word in conformity with the Spirit of God living in you.

The Spirit in you bears witness to the AGAPE LOVE of God living in you.

Jesus Christ legally and judicially restored you back to your legal family as a Child of God as a spirit Being. You have all the legal rights and privileges as a son or daughter of God. You are a spirit Being made in the image and likeness of God in Christ Jesus.

3

Sin Conscious

"Fraud" Day 3

First published September 25, 2018 in the Fraud Series – The Repple Minute

Day 3 of the Fraud committed by Satan against man

Sin Conscious

Satan committed fraud in the Garden of Eden by stealing Man's identity of Righteousness in right standing with God. Man has a legal and judicial right to be restored back into right standing with God in Righteousness.

Satan perverted the truth of man's righteousness and holiness in order to induce man to be sin conscious.

> "For the worshipers, having once [for all time] been cleansed, would no longer have a **consciousness of sin**."
> - *Hebrews 10:2b AMP*

"For God made Christ, who never sinned, to be the offering for our sin, so that we could be made right with God through Christ."
- *2 Corinthians 5:21 NLT*

Jesus Christ's sacrifice on the cross removed the sins for all mankind forever to those who receive and accept God's Agape love gift in Christ Jesus. HIS Gift has brought those who are born again into right standing with God. You are made righteous and HOLY and able to enter into the Presence of Holy God. Not by anything you have done but by what Christ Jesus did through HIS shed Blood for you and all.

God does not see your sin. HE sees Jesus. Satan's intentional fraud is to steal your legal right to being RIGHTEOUS and HOLY in Christ Jesus. Satan wants his followers to be sin conscious.

Jesus Christ purged all of mankind's sin forever. God sees you as righteous and Holy. HIS sacrifice through HIS Death is a once and for all removal of ALL sin forever.

Satan perpetrates his fraud by getting mankind to believe they can only enter into God's presence by being good through performance not the shed blood of Jesus Christ. The truth is that performance has nothing to do with your being able to enter into the presence of HOLY GOD.

You are able to enter into the presence of God based upon the sacrifice of Jesus Christ, not animals on the altar or your performance. It is the once and for all sacrifice of the Blood of Jesus Christ.

Jesus Christ legally and judicially restored you back to your legal family as a Child of God in right standing with God. You have all the legal rights and privileges as a son or daughter of God. You are the Righteousness of God in Christ Jesus. You are Righteousness Conscious.

You are given a perfect, cleaned and righteous conscious washed by the blood of Jesus Christ.

> "How much more will the blood of Christ, who through the eternal [Holy] Spirit *willingly* offered Himself unblemished [that is, without moral or spiritual imperfection as a sacrifice] to God, cleanse your conscience from dead works *and* lifeless observances to serve the ever living God?" *Hebrews 9:14*

Your debt of sin has been paid. It is like your mortgage and financial debts have been paid. You don't need to be conscious of your debt anymore. You have been set free and are no longer in bondage to the financial debt. Your sin has been forgiven, removed and forgotten in Christ Jesus forever. You are purged of your sin. You no longer need to be sin conscious but conscious of your standing in the family of God in Christ Jesus as a dearly loved child.

Your heavenly Father AGAPE loves you so much HE paid your debt.

"And in accordance with this will [of God], we have been made holy (consecrated and sanctified) through the offering made once for all of the body of Jesus Christ (the Anointed One)."

- *Hebrews 10:10*

You have been made HOLY and SANCTIFIED through the offering of Jesus Christ. You are RIGHTEOUSNESS Conscience in Christ Jesus.

4

Injustice

"Fraud" Day 4

First published September 26, 2018 in the Fraud Series – The Repple Minute

Day 4 of the Fraud committed by Satan against man

Injustice

Satan committed fraud in the Garden of Eden by stealing Man's identity of Justice to be in right standing with God.

> "Righteousness and justice are the foundation of Your throne; mercy *and* loving-kindness and truth go before Your face."
> - *Psalm 89:14 AMP*

The foundation of God's throne is righteousness and justice. Justice flows from God's heart. God's AGAPE love and kindness go before you in truth. God is not angry at you.

The nature of Satan is **injustice**. God gave dominion to Adam and Eve over earth while Satan is mad over being kicked out of heaven. You have been imputed with Satan's injustice, anger, bitterness, selfishness, regret and unforgiveness because of the fall through Adam and Eve.

One of Satan's tools is to get you focused on your **unjust circumstance** instead of God's AGAPE love, mercy and grace found in your redemption and the resurrection power of Jesus Christ. The resurrection power of Christ living in you defeats injustice. Jesus Christ took all injustice in HIS DEATH on the cross and declared that it is finished. HIS JUSTICE and RIGHTEOUSNESS was imputed to man and Jesus took all man's sin and injustice. This is the great unequal exchange: HIS RIGHTEOUSNESS for our sin.

Satan is a liar. He wants you to believe and trust your **injustice**.

Have you invited injustice into your heart? Are you living beneath what God has planned for you because of carrying injustice in your heart?

Satan came to kill, steal and destroy you. He does not want you healthy, he does not want you to be celebrating in your salvation, and he does not want you to have the peace which passes all understanding.

Here is a list of things which the enemy Satan wants you to think on:

- All the unjust acts brought against you in word and deed
- All the wrong things you have done
- All your inadequacies and insecurities
- All your hurts, wrongs and unjust acts against you
- All the shame, guilt, regret, fear, and lack these unjust acts caused you
- You deserve more and better treatment
- You were treated wrongly and need justice (man's justice)

God's throne is Righteousness and Justice which was imputed to you in Christ Jesus. You are forgiven and made righteous. Jesus Christ took your judgment on the cross and paid to bring you into right standing with your FATHER. You have been judged and the verdict is "NOT GUILTY." You are the righteousness of God in Christ Jesus.

Are you going to trust and believe in the finished judicial and righteous work of God's AGAPE love or trust Satan's scheme of injustice?

Jesus Christ legally and judicially restored you back to your legal family as a Child of God in right standing with God. You have all the legal rights and privileges as a son or daughter of God. You are the Righteousness of God in Christ Jesus. You are justified in Christ Jesus.

5

Rejection

"Fraud" Day 5

First published September 27, 2018 in the Fraud Series — The Repple Minute

Day 5 of the Fraud committed by Satan against man

Rejection

Satan is the father and author of rejection. Satan wants you to live with rejection and injustice. Satan was rejected as an archangel. When you are feeling and exhibiting rejection, you are following the devil's scheme.

The devil is rejected out of heaven. He is defeated by the blood of the lamb, the word of your testimony and by your willingness to not love your life and not renounce your faith even when faced with death.

"And they overcame *and* conquered him because of the blood of the Lamb and because of the word of their testimony, for they did not love their life *and* renounce their faith even when faced with death."
- *Revelations 12:11 AMP*

In Matthew 4:10, Jesus rejects Satan and tells him to "get out of here."

"**Get out of here, Satan**," Jesus told him. "For the Scriptures say, 'You must worship the LORD your God and serve only him.'"
- *Matthew 4:10*

You have victory over Satan's schemes. However, you are following Satan;

- when you reject God's AGAPE love,

- when you reject that all your sin has been forgiven, past, present and future,

- when you reject your identity in Christ as "the righteousness of God in Christ Jesus" and a "Child of God,"

- when you reject all God has for you,

- when you reject the complete finished work on the cross,

- when you reject HIS forgiveness,

- when you reject HIS WORD.

God cannot reject you because HE has totally accepted you. Man cannot reject you because he has not accepted you. Only God is the one who can accept you. You cannot be rejected by someone who has not accepted you.

Only **you can reject God** and HIS GIFT of RIGHTEOUSNESS through HIS Son Jesus Christ.

This is another scheme of the devil - to seek acceptance from man versus God. You will always be following Satan if you are seeking the acceptance of man.

God has already accepted you and shown HIS DIVINE AGAPE LOVE for mankind through HIS SON Jesus Christ. HIS AGAPE love was demonstrated on the cross through the shed blood of Jesus Christ.

Jesus Christ legally and judicially restored you back to your legal family as a Child of God in right standing with God. You have all the legal rights and privileges as a son or daughter of God. You are the Righteousness of God in Christ Jesus. You are accepted not rejected in Christ Jesus.

6

Truth

"Fraud" Day 6

First published September 28, 2018 in the Fraud Series – The Repple Minute

Day 6 of the Fraud committed by Satan against man

Truth

Satan committed fraud in the Garden of Eden by stealing the Truth of God. Man exchanged Truth of God for the lies of Satan. Man has a legal and judicial right to be restored back into right standing with God in Truth.

What is the standard by which you measure reality and truth?

Truth is the absolute standard by which reality is measured not your perception of reality.

The Truth is that Jesus is Lord. There is a Kingdom of God. Jesus said to seek first the Kingdom of God and HIS RIGHTEOUSNESS. There is a Kingdom of God economy.

Jesus came to earth to bring the Kingdom of God to live in mankind through the Holy Spirit. Jesus came to redeem mankind back to their original value.

> "You are a king, then!" said Pilate. Jesus answered, "You are right in saying I am a king. In fact, for this reason I was born, and for this I came into the world, to testify to the truth. Everyone on the side of truth listens to me."
> - *John 18:37*

> "Jesus answered, "I am the way and the truth and the life. No one comes to the Father except through me.""
> - *John 14:6*

Feelings are real but your feelings are not truth. Your feelings of fear are real but not truth. Your feelings of anger and bitterness are real but not truth.

You've probably heard the statement "perception is reality." Yet your perception is not truth.

Satan is a liar. He is deceptive. He wants your perception and feeling of reality to become your truth rather than for you to know the real TRUTH of the person of Jesus Christ.

Satan does not want you to know the truth. Here are some truths:

Jesus Christ came to earth to destroy the works of the enemy. HE came to bring truth. HE came to redeem you from the lies and deception of this world. HE came to bring you abundant life which is victory over sin, death, condemnation, guilt, fear, shame, regret and your feelings.

Jesus Christ came to give you power, AGAPE love and a sound mind in HIS HOLY SPIRIT living in your Temple. HIS power is greater than cancer. HIS power is greater than sickness. HIS power is greater than injustice. HIS power is full of love, forgiveness, restoration and redemption. HE restores you into the image in which you were created. HE is LORD. HE is worthy of your worship and praise. HIS promises are true. HE is the EVERLASTING KING. HE is the ruler of the universe. HE AGAPE loves you unconditionally. You are HIS BELOVED child.

Jesus Christ legally and judicially restored you back to your legal family as a Child of God in right standing with God. You have all the legal rights and privileges as a son or daughter of God. You are the Righteousness of God in Christ Jesus. You have the Truth of God living in you through the Holy Spirit.

7

Complaints

"Fraud" Day 7

First published October 1, 2018 in the Fraud Series – The Repple Minute

Day 7 of the Fraud committed by Satan against man

Complaints

Satan committed fraud in the Garden of Eden by stealing Man's identity as a Child of God. Man has a legal and judicial right to be restored back to the image and likeness of God. Satan is making complaints and claims against you.

A claim is an accusation or assertion which may be brought against you. Attorneys make claims/complaints for their client against their opponent. Often the attorney's complaint is filled with fictitious facts against you which are not the TRUTH.

Here are some claims against you by the attorney Satan. This attorney wants you to be filled with fear and believe the complaints/claims against you.

Complaint 1. God does not like you. God is angry at you.

Complaint 2. God does not love you.

Complaint 3. God made you this way filled with anger, bitterness and unforgiveness.

Complaint 4. You will never get out of debt. You will always be a debtor.

Complaint 5. You are not loved or accepted by your spouse, family, friends and associates.

Complaint 6. All the bad things which have happened are your fault. You should be ashamed.

Complaint 7. You have a right to get even with people who have mistreated you.

Complaint 8. You will get heart disease, diabetes and/or Alzheimer's because it runs in my family.

Complaint 9. You will be an alcoholic because it runs in my family.

Complaint 10. Your parents, brothers and sisters and boss mistreated you.

Complaint 11. You do not have enough money. You will never retire.

Complaint 12. You will never amount to anything. You are not good enough.

Complaint 13. You are going to die.

Complaint 14. You need to give up pursuing your dream you will never be successful.

The attorney is shouting complaints, curses and claims against you which reside in your thinking. Some of the claims may be facts, however they are not the TRUTH about what God says about you. God's claims about you are greater than the claims of Satan. You have a New Nature in Christ Jesus. Jesus Christ is the truth. Jesus came to set you free from the works/thinking of the enemy. Jesus has given you victory through his death, burial and resurrection to free you from the claims of the Satan. You are no longer under the curse but the blessing.

> "So, if the Son sets you free, you will be free indeed."
> - *John 8:36*

> "Who gave (yielded) Himself up [to atone] for our sins [and to save and sanctify us], in order to rescue *and* **deliver us from this present wicked** age *and* world order, in accordance with the will *and* purpose *and* plan of our God and Father."
> - *Galatians 1:4 AMP*

You have been made righteous through Jesus Christ. You are not under the curse or claims of Satan against you. You are not guilty in Christ Jesus.

"God made him who had no sin to be sin for us, so that in him we might become the **righteousness of God**."

-   *2 Corinthians 5:21*

Jesus Christ legally and judicially restored you back to your legal family as a Child of God. All claims and complaints have been dismissed. You have all the legal rights and privileges as a son or daughter of God. You have been adjudicated not guilty from any of the complaints and claims against you by the blood of Jesus Christ.

8

Blessing

"Fraud" Day 8

First published October 2, 2018 in the Fraud Series – The Repple Minute

Day 8 of the Fraud committed by Satan against man

Blessing

"²⁷ So God created man in His own image, in the image *and* likeness of God He created him; male and female He created them. ²⁸ And **God blessed them** [granting them certain authority] and said to them, "Be fruitful, multiply, and fill the earth, and subjugate it [putting it under your power]; and rule over (dominate) the fish of the sea, the birds of the air, and every living thing that moves upon the earth.""
- *Genesis 1: 27-28 AMP*

"Today I have given you the choice between life and death, between **blessings and curses.** Now I call on heaven and earth to witness the choice you make. Oh, that you would choose life, so that you and your descendants might live!"
-   *Deuteronomy 30:19*

There is power in the spoken word. God spoke creation into existence and Blessed Man with spoken words.

"The tongue has the power of life and death, and those who love it will eat its fruit."
-   *Proverbs 18:21 NIV*

There are consequences to your spoken words. You will reap what you speak. You will eat the fruit of your life-giving words of love, repentance, encouragement, forgiveness, correction, rebuke and **Blessing.** The Blessing brings restoration, reconciliation and RIGHTEOUSNESS in right standing with God.

You will also eat of the words coming out of your mouth spoken in jealousy, anger, rage, bitterness, hatred, envy and cursing.

These words stop the Blessing of the Devine Favor of God being released through you.

The choice is yours. You can choose to think, believe, speak, and be Blessed. The Lord tells HIS CHILDREN to choose life which is Blessed.

As a born-again child of God, your current sorrow or grief will deliver you from evil (curse) to bring you salvation (Blessed) and hope in Christ Jesus as your Lord.

Jesus Christ legally and judicially restored you back to your legal family as a Child of God with **the Blessing**. You have all the legal rights and privileges as a son or daughter of God. You have the same Blessing of Adam in the Garden. The same Blessing of Abraham, the same Blessing of Jesus with the Holy Spirit living in you.

9

Steal

"Fraud" Day 9

First published October 3, 2018 in the Fraud Series – The Repple Minute

Day 9 of the Fraud committed by Satan against man

Steal

Satan is a liar and thief. Satan committed fraud in the Garden of Eden by stealing the man's knowledge and relationship with God. Man exchanged Truth of God for the lies of Satan. Man has a legal and judicial right to be restored back into right standing with God in Truth.

The following are some of the strategies the thief, Satan, uses to attack and destroy your thinking.

For the Born-Again believer, the Spirit of God which entered into you is the same Holy Spirit which raised Jesus from the dead and dwelled in Peter and Paul.

However, your mind, will and emotions (soul) have not been redeemed. Your mind, will and emotions need to be renewed and surrendered to the Holy Spirit. Your mind is the place that Satan attacks, therefore every thought needs to be taken captive by the Word of God.

Identify who wants you to think a certain way - is it Satan or God in the following statements?

Who wants you to think the Bible, God, Jesus, Noah, Joseph, Daniel and David are fables and stories which are not true?

Who wants you to think what you see is more important than the unseen?

Who wants you to trust in your own intellect, senses and reasoning rather than think there is a Creator, Redeemer God?

Who is the liar and accuser of the brethren?

Who wants to deceive your mind and thinking by making you think what is evil is good and what is good is evil?

Who wants you to focus on lack of wealth, success and position?

Who wants you to think that you should **not** be wealthy?

Who wants you to be sick and filled with disease?

Who wants you to **not** forgive and hold a grudge against your spouse, kids, sibling, parents, boss, co-worker?

Who wants you to think you have been mistreated and injustice has happened in your life?

Who wants you to be filled with anger, bitterness, blame, revenge and unforgiveness?

Who wants you to think you need the love of man or woman to be accepted?

Who wants you to think the good life is partying, drinking, drugs and sexual behavior outside of marriage?

Who wants you to live with no condemnation knowing all your sins past, present and future HE will remember no more?

Who wants you to know you are AGAPE LOVED and even demonstrated HIS AGAPE LOVE?

Who wants you to know HE came to destroy the works of the enemy of lack, fear, death, sickness, insufficiency, inadequacy and hopelessness?

Who wants you to know every need is met that you will ever have?

Who wants you to live with power, AGAPE love and a sound mind?

Who wants you to know you will never have lack?

Who wants you to know you have been made RIGHTEOUS NOW?

Who wants you to know you enter God's Presence based upon what Jesus did, not based upon your behavior?

Who wants you to know HE is GOOD and AGAPE LOVES so much that HE GAVE?

Who wants you to know you have been redeemed, restored and lives in you?

Who wants you to know you are made in HIS IMAGE and LIKENESS which is SPIRIT?

Who wants you to have HIS MIND?

Who wants you to receive the complete Gift of Salvation and the Gift of Righteousness?

Jesus Christ legally and judicially restored you back to your legal family as a Child of God as a Spirit Being. You have all the legal rights and privileges as a son or daughter of God. You have LIFE ABUNDANTLY. You are made in the image and likeness of God in Christ Jesus. You have the mind Christ and the Wisdom of God living in you.

10

Identity

"Fraud" Day 10

First published October 4, 2018 in the Fraud Series – The Repple Minute

Day 10 of the Fraud committed by Satan against man

Identity

Satan committed fraud in the Garden of Eden by stealing Man's Identity. Man has a legal and judicial right to be restored back to their identity which is the image and likeness of God.

You are made like God!!!!

"**26** Then God said, "Let Us (Father, Son, Holy Spirit) make man in Our image, according to Our likeness [not physical, but a spiritual personality and moral likeness]; and let them have complete authority over the fish of the sea, the birds of the air, the cattle, and over the entire earth, and over everything that creeps *and* crawls on the earth."

27 So God created man in His own image, in the image *and* likeness of God He created him; male and female He created them."
- *Genesis 1:26-27 AMP*

Your original identity is in the image and likeness of the Godhead. You are made in the image and likeness of the Father, Son and Holy Spirit.

You are made like God!!!!

But Satan has stolen your identity.

Satan is a liar and full of deceit. Satan's big scheme is for you to doubt your identity. Satan wants to steal your identity with doubt that you cannot be like God. Adam and Eve were already like God made in HIS image and likeness. Yet here is Satan's scheme to Adam and Eve: Being like God is something they can achieve by eating from the tree. "You will be like God," Satan said. Their identity was already in God's likeness and image. This is not something they needed to achieve and become.

"⁴ Then the serpent said to the woman, "You will not surely die. ⁵ For God knows that in the day you eat of it your eyes will be opened, and **you will be like God**, knowing good and evil.""
- *Genesis 3:4-5 NKJV*

Satan is after your identity.

God has already told you that you are made in GOD's IMAGE and LIKENESS. God's LOVE was demonstrated in Christ Jesus to redeem you into HIS IMAGE and LIKENESS. God is love. You are made in GOD's image and likeness of LOVE.

You are made like the Father, Son and Holy Spirit.

The same resurrection power which raised Jesus from the dead is living in you NOW!

Your created design and purpose is the image and likeness of God. You are made like God as a LOVE being. Receive and believe your RIGHTEOUS standing in Christ Jesus knowing you are a son and daughter of GOD.

Jesus Christ legally and judicially restored you back to your legal family as a Child of God in the image and likeness of God. You have all the legal rights and privileges as a son or daughter of God. You are BLESSED.

11

Lie

"Fraud" Day 11

First published October 5, 2018 in the Fraud Series – The Repple Minute

Day 11 of the Fraud committed by Satan against man

Lie

The devil does not want you to understand Hebrews 10. The big lie of the devil is he wants you to believe that God will remind you of all your sins, mistakes, bad deeds, broken promises, bad words spoken and everything you did wrong. The devil wants you to think that God has a big computer which keeps track of every wrong you ever did. This is a big lie for those who have accepted Jesus Christ as Lord with a (new nature). The devil wants you to have a guilty conscience (old nature).

- "¹⁴ For by a single offering He has **forever completely cleansed** *and* **perfected** those who are consecrated *and* made holy."

- "¹⁷ He then goes on to say, "And their **sins and their lawbreaking I will <u>remember no more</u>.**""

- "¹⁸ Now where there is absolute remission (forgiveness and cancellation of the penalty) of these [sins and lawbreaking], there is no longer any offering made to atone for sin."

- "²² Let us all come forward *and* draw near with true (honest and sincere) hearts in unqualified assurance *and* absolute conviction engendered by faith (by that leaning of the entire human personality on God in absolute trust and confidence in His power, wisdom, and goodness), having our hearts sprinkled *and* purified from a **guilty (evil) conscience** and our **bodies cleansed with pure water**."
  - *Hebrews 10:14,17-18, 22 AMP*

The enemy of God is a liar. The devil wants God's people to live in defeat, sickness, emptiness, fear, unforgiveness, bitterness, anger, blame, lack, and without hope.

The devil **does not** want you to walk by faith. He wants you to trust in your own ways and trust your human logic and reasoning. He does not want you to be bold in:

- Your confession that "you are the Righteousness of God in Christ Jesus."

- Your confession that "you have no condemnation because you are in Christ Jesus and HE is in you."

- Your confession that "you have been redeemed, healed, restored and reconciled to God in Christ Jesus."

- Your confession that "you are beloved and blessed by the blood of Jesus Christ."

The devil wants you to live in fear of judgement. Jesus Christ took all your judgment and wrath on the cross. God looks to Jesus, not you, for your redemption. God will not remember your sins. You have been cleansed and purified. You have been made Righteous by the blood of Jesus Christ. Jesus removed your guilty conscience and replaced it with his righteousness.

Jesus Christ legally and judicially restored you back to your legal family as a Child of God in the image and likeness of God. You have all the legal rights and privileges as a son or daughter of God. You are blessed. You are designed to operate at the level of your father. You have life abundantly. You have the mind of Christ and the wisdom of God living in you.

12

Behavior

"Fraud" Day 12

First published October 8, 2018 in the Fraud Series – The Repple Minute

Day 12 of the Fraud committed by Satan against man

Behavior

Your behavior does not determine your identity and destiny. This is a lie from the accuser of the brethren, the devil. Your identity and destiny is determined by a person: either **Adam** or the finished work of **Jesus Christ.**

Does your sin make you a sinner? You are a sinner because of a person, Adam. You have been redeemed, restored, justified (made righteous), saved, healed and made complete by the finished work of the person Jesus Christ on the cross.

"Look at what you did" is the accusation from the accuser of the brethren. He stands before the heavenly courts of God accusing mankind of his wicked deeds and sinful behavior.

"You deserve punishment" is what the accuser in the heavenly courts says. The accuser brings complaints for your wrongdoing from the past. He accuses you and all mankind of your behavior. "Look at what you did. You deserve to be punished. You are guilty." This causes you to live in guilt, shame, fear and condemnation.

However, your advocate in court is Jesus Christ. He is your defense attorney. He stands up in court and admits that all these behaviors and actions the accused did commit. However, "I (Jesus Christ the advocate) have paid and taken the penalty for these actions and even the future actions for the accused."

It is up to the Judge to rule. All the evidence is presented to the Judge by the accuser of the brethren (Prosecuting Attorney) and The Great High Priest and Advocate Jesus Christ (Defense Attorney). The verdict is finally read and a Declaration of Judgment is made by God (the Judge).

The verdict is NOT GUILTY because Jesus Christ made the payment. All records will be expunged and removed as if nothing had ever happened.

The declaratory judgment reads that because of the penalty being paid by the blood of Jesus Christ on the Cross, there is no guilt, shame, condemnation, fear or worry of your wrong. You will never again go to trial. The case is totally dismissed forever.

Your new identity is the "Righteousness of God in Christ Jesus."

> *2 Corinthians 5:21* "God made him who had no sin to be sin for us, so that in him **we might become the righteousness of God.**"

Jesus Christ legally and judicially restored you back to your legal family as a Child of God in the image and likeness of God. You have all the legal rights and privileges as a son or daughter of God. You are BLESSED. You have life abundantly. You have the mind of Christ and the Wisdom of God living in you.

13

Wisdom

"Fraud" Day 13

First published October 9, 2018 in the Fraud Series – The Repple Minute

Day 13 of the Fraud committed by Satan against man

Wisdom

Satan committed fraud in the Garden of Eden by stealing the wisdom of God from man. Man became limited to his five senses and his own intellect. Man has a legal and judicial right to be restored back to their identity with the wisdom of God and having unlimited communication with God.

> "For whoever **has** will be given more, and they will have an abundance. Whoever **does not have**, even what they have will be taken from them."
> -   *Matthew 25:29*

What is the **HAS**?

Why did Jesus speak in parables? The answer to this question will reveal what is the **HAS**.

> "**¹⁰** Then the disciples came to Him and asked, "Why do You speak to the crowds in parables?" **¹¹** Jesus replied to them, "To you it has been granted to know the mysteries of the kingdom of heaven, but to them it has not been granted.**¹²** For **whoever has** [spiritual wisdom because he is receptive to God's word], to him *more* **will be given**, and he will be richly *and* abundantly supplied; but whoever does not have [**spiritual wisdom because he has devalued God's word**], even what he has will be taken away from him. **¹³** This is the reason I speak to the crowds in parables: because while [having the power of] seeing they do not see, and while [having the power of] hearing they do not hear, nor do they understand *and* grasp [spiritual things]." - *Matthew 13:10-13*

Jesus used parables to teach about HIS KINGDOM. **Has** is spiritual wisdom. Then Jesus said to them, "If you can't understand the meaning of this parable, how will you understand all the other parables?" Mark 4:13 NLT. Without **spiritual wisdom**, the mysteries of the Kingdom of heaven will stay locked.

King Solomon unlocked this Kingdom principle:

> "10 "**Give me <u>wisdom</u> and knowledge**, that I may lead this people, for who is able to govern this great people of yours?" 11 God said to Solomon, "Since this is your **<u>heart's desire</u>** and you have not asked for wealth, possessions or honor, nor for the death of your enemies, and since you have not asked for a long life but for wisdom and knowledge to govern my people over whom I have made you king, 12 therefore **<u>wisdom</u>** and knowledge will be given you. And I will also give you wealth, possessions and honor, such as no king who was before you ever had and none after you will have.""
> - *2 Chronicles 1:10-12*

> "24 "So everyone who **hears these words** of Mine and acts on them, will **be like a <u>wise</u> man** [a far-sighted, practical, and sensible man] who built his house on the rock. 25 And the rain fell, and the floods *and* torrents came, and the winds blew and slammed against that house; yet it did not fall, because it had been **founded on the rock**. 26 And everyone who hears these words of Mine and **does not do them**, will be **like a foolish** (stupid) man who built his house on the sand. 27 And the rain fell, and the floods *and* torrents came, and the winds blew and slammed against that house; and it fell—and great *and* complete was its fall.""
> - *Matthew 7:24-27 AMP*

The **has** is putting into practice the wisdom found coming from God's Word.

 Jesus Christ legally and judicially restored you back to your legal family as a Child of God with the Wisdom of God. You have all the legal rights and privileges as a son or daughter of God. You are BLESSED.

> "If any of you lacks wisdom, let him ask of God, who gives to all liberally and without reproach, and it will be given to him."
> - *James 1:5 NKJV*

14

Position

"Fraud" Day 14

First published October 10, 2018 in the Fraud Series – The Repple Minute

Day 14 of the Fraud committed by Satan against man

Position

Satan committed fraud in the Garden of Eden by stealing man's position with God. Man has a legal and judicial right to be restored back to his position in right standing with God.

> "But you are a chosen people, a royal priesthood, a holy nation, a people belonging to God, that you may declare the praises of him who called you out of darkness into HIS wonderful light. Once you were not a people, but now you are the people of God; once you had not received mercy, but now you have received mercy."
> *1 Peter 2:9-10*

You are a chosen people. You are God's chosen race of people. This is not based upon physical descendants but by grace of God through Jesus Christ to all HIS chosen believers.

You are a Royal Priesthood. God had a purpose for the Nation of Israel and so HE brought them out of slavery in Egypt. These people were called to be a nation of priests who would represent God and his plan for the salvation of humanity. As the Father's elected you are a Royal Priesthood called to these same responsibilities. You are called to bring the Good News of the Gospel of Jesus Christ, HIS righteousness, redemption, forgiveness and grace to the dark and lost world.

You are a Holy Nation. Jesus as the King of kings presides over the citizens of the Holy Nation on earth. Jesus is responsible for the care and protection of his Father's elected children as their King, elder brother, and high priest.

You are a people belonging to God. Once you were not a people of God. You were once in rebellion against God, but now because of God's mercy through the shed blood of Jesus you have come out of darkness into light and belong to God. God wants all the blessings of God to flow to HIS children.

You sing and praise God because you have been brought out of darkness into HIS light. HE is in you and you are in HIM. You sing because you are free from sin and death. The joy of the Lord is your strength. God's mercy is on you. You deserved death as the penalty for your sin but because of God's mercy for you through Jesus Christ you have received the pardon and forgiveness of your sin. The penalty for sin is death and the gift of God is eternal life through Jesus Christ.

Jesus Christ legally and judicially restored you back to your legal family as a Child of God in the image and likeness of God. You have all the legal rights and privileges as a son or daughter of God. You are BLESSED. You have life abundantly. You have the mind of Christ and the Wisdom of God living in you.

15

Mammon

"Fraud" Day 15

First published October 11, 2018 in the Fraud Series – The Repple Minute

Day 15 of the Fraud committed by Satan against man

Mammon

Merriam-Webster defines fraud as follows: intentional perversion of truth in order to induce another to part with something of value or to surrender a legal right.

Satan stole man's legal right to the abundance of wealth of this world. Satan is controlling the wealth of this world for his purpose through his people and has perverted mankind to think with a poverty and scarcity mindset.

Mammon is crying out to be redeemed.

What is mammon? Mammon comes from the Syrian god of riches, the god of finances and wealth. The god of mammon is worshipped. It means something you can put your trust in, something you can lean on for your life. It also means greed. It means riches.

Money is crying out to be redeemed into the hands of the RIGHTEOUS. Mammon is crying out to be under the dominion of the Children of Righteousness.

> "The wealth of the sinner is stored up for the Righteous."
> - *Proverbs 13:22*

> "No man can serve two masters: for either he will hate the one, and love the other; or else he will hold to the one, and despise the other. Ye cannot serve God and mammon."
> - *Matthew 6:24*

Here is what the Spirit of Mammon says:

- (Mammon) says you don't need God, I can offer you everything which God offers you.

- (Mammon) says you can have financial freedom with me.

- (Mammon) says you can be independent with me.

- (Mammon) says you will have power with me.

- (Mammon) says you can have security and safety with more of me.

- (Mammon) says you will be respected and have significance if you have more of me.

- (Mammon) says you can trust me.

- (Mammon) says you don't have enough of me.

- (Mammon) says you need more and you deserve more.

- (Mammon) says you will have comfort and contentment with more of me.

- (Mammon) says you don't want to lose me.

Money is neutral. However, the Spirit of Mammon is demonic and seeks control over your life. Money in the hands of the Children of RIGHTEOUS is used to further the Kingdom of God.

Jesus Christ is all you need. HE redeemed you, saved you, healed you, restored you, forgave you and reconciled you back to your FATHER. HE is the only one who can offer you victory over the spirit of mammon, the spirit of scarcity, the spirit of poverty, condemnation, death, and fear. HE is the only one who gives you right standing with God (RIGHTEOUSNESS). You are the RIGHTEUOSNESS of GOD in CHRIST JESUS.

Put your trust in God who gave HIS only son as a Gift to make your RIGHTEOUS so that you can have all God's inheritance? Money is crying out to be redeemed by the RIGTHEOUS.

Jesus Christ legally and judicially restored you back to your legal family as a Child of God in the image and likeness of God. You have all the legal rights and privileges as a son or daughter of God. You are BLESSED. You have life abundantly. You have the mind of Christ and the Wisdom of God living in you.

16

Accused

"Fraud" Day 16

First published October 12, 2018 in the Fraud Series – The Repple Minute

Day 16 of the Fraud committed by Satan against man

Accused

Satan committed fraud in the Garden of Eden deceiving man to disobey God. Because of man's disobedience, the unrenewed mind continues to accuse, condemn and bring complaints about its unworthiness.

> "But you belong to God, my dear children. You have already won a victory over those people, because the **Spirit who lives in you is greater than the spirit who lives in the world.**"
> - *1 John 4:4 NLT*

"²Do not be conformed to this world (this age), [fashioned after and adapted to its external, superficial customs], but **be transformed (changed) by the [entire] renewal of your mind [by its new ideals and its new attitude],** so that you may prove [for yourselves] what is the good and acceptable and perfect will of God, *even* the thing which is good and acceptable and perfect [in His sight for you]."
- *Romans 12:2 AMPC*

Good news! You are the Temple of the Living God, and the Holy Spirit is living and dwelling in you with God's word flowing through your innermost being like springs and rivers of living water. Your soul is being continually washed by the Blood of Jesus 24/7 bringing you into a righteous consciousness.

"¹*There is* therefore now no condemnation to those who are in Christ Jesus, who do not walk according to the flesh, but according to the Spirit. ² For the law of the Spirit of life in Christ Jesus has made me free from the law of sin and death."
- *Romans 8:1-2 NKJV*

When you are walking according to the spirit your mind will be renewed. You are set free from all the complaints, attacks, accusations, lies and condemnation brought against you.

"The Spirit Himself [thus] testifies together with our own spirit, [assuring us] that we are children of God."
- *Romans 8:16 AMPC*

Walk today in the freedom knowing you are not condemned because you walk by the spirit and not by the flesh. You have the mind of Christ.

God made HIM who knew no sin to become sin, so that you can be restored into the RIGHTEOUSNESS of GOD in Christ Jesus.

Jesus Christ legally and judicially restored you back to your legal family as a Child of God in the image and likeness of God. You have all the legal rights and privileges as a son or daughter of God. You are BLESSED. You have life abundantly. You have the mind of Christ and the Wisdom of God living in you.

17

Self-Confident

"Fraud" Day 17

First published October 15, 2018 in the Fraud Series – The Repple Minute

Day 17 of the Fraud committed by Satan against man

Self-Confident

Satan committed fraud in the Garden of Eden wanting man to be self-confident and trust in themselves instead of God.

We have been trained by the lies and standards of this world which is to be self-confident. How is it working being self-confident? Has trusting in your own confidence removed, fear, worry, guilt, condemnation, regret, rejection, loneliness, hurt, anger, depression and unforgiveness? By putting your confidence in yourself, have you gained victory over your emotions, worries and feelings?

The Word of God is contrary to the world's way of thinking.

> *Proverbs 3:5-7* "Trust in the Lord with all your heart, and lean not on your own understanding; In all your ways acknowledge Him, And he shall direct your paths. Do not be wise in your own eyes; fear the Lord and depart from evil."

> *Romans 12:2* "And do not be conformed to this world, but be transformed by the renewing of your mind, that you may prove what is that good and acceptable and perfect will of God."

- The transformed mind is renewed into the image and likeness of God's love.

- The transformed mind knows their identity in Christ Jesus.

- The transformed mind knows God's love and total forgiveness of sin.

- The transformed mind knows they are the Righteousness of God in Christ Jesus.

The perfect will of God is found when you trust God with all of your heart, mind, soul, and strength. HIS perfect will is a choice of your will to seek HIM. When you seek HIM you will find HIM, when you seek HIM with all of your heart.

"If any of you lacks wisdom [to guide him through a decision or circumstance], he is to **ask of [our benevolent] God**, who **gives to** <u>everyone</u> <u>generously</u> and without rebuke *or* blame, and it will be given to him."
- James 1:5 AMP

The Holy Spirit lives in the born-again follower of Christ Jesus. Your confidence in God's Word and HIS Wisdom will give you victory over your circumstances and problems. Jesus Christ's resurrection has given you victory over sin and death. Seek first HIS KINGDOM versus your kingdom and your paths will be made straight.

Jesus Christ legally and judicially restored you back to your legal family as a Child of God in the image and likeness of God. You have all the legal rights and privileges as a son or daughter of God. You are BLESSED. You have life abundantly. You have the mind of Christ and the Wisdom of God living in you.

18

Deliverance

"Fraud" Day 18

First published October 16, 2018 in the Fraud Series — The Repple Minute

Day 18 of the Fraud committed by Satan against man

Deliverance

Satan committed fraud in the Garden of Eden. Since then, mankind has been under Satanic Rule in this world which brings, sickness, death, lack, guilt, shame, condemnation, fear, worry, anxiety, heaviness, temporal, and selfishness.

> "[9] because if you **acknowledge** *and* **confess** with your **mouth** that **Jesus is Lord** [recognizing His power, authority, and majesty as God], and **believe in your heart** that God raised Him from the dead, you will be saved.

¹⁰ For with the heart a person believes [in Christ as Savior] resulting in his justification [that is, **being made righteous—being freed of the guilt of sin and made acceptable to God**]; and with the mouth he acknowledges *and* confesses [his faith openly], resulting in *and* confirming [his] salvation."
- *Romans 10:9-10 AMP*

God's New Creation delivered and redeemed all mankind into the image and likeness of God through Jesus Christ. Your redemption in Christ Jesus has delivered you out of the Satanic Rule into the Kingdom of God. Christ lives in you through the Holy Spirit. You are delivered into the abundant life. You are delivered into the Agape Love of God. You are delivered over the power of sin and death. You are set free from the bondage of this world in Christ Jesus. You are delivered into the Shalom Peace of God. You are delivered into the Fatherhood of God.

You have been justified and made righteous so that you can enter **Boldly** into the Presence of God, just like you had never sinned. All your selfishness, guilt, shame and sin past, present and future has been removed by the Blood of Jesus Christ.

You are the Righteousness of God in Christ Jesus! You have been delivered into God's Presence as a son and daughter with all the legal rights as a Child of God to use the Name of Jesus with all authority by your Heavenly Father.

Jesus Christ legally and judicially restored you back to your legal family as a Child of God in the image and likeness of God. You have all the legal rights and privileges as a son or daughter of God. You are BLESSED. You have life abundantly. You have the mind of Christ and the Wisdom of God living in you.

19

Orphan Spirit

"Fraud" Day 19

First published October 17, 2018 in the Fraud Series – The Repple Minute

Day 19 of the Fraud committed by Satan against man

Orphan Spirit

The rebellion and fall of man caused by Adam has put a longing in your heart to be adopted and restored to your Daddy, Father God. You want the love of Daddy, you desire the Father's love. You are born looking for HIS love which can only be found through Jesus Christ.

You have looked to your earthly parents to fulfill this void which is deep in your heart and yearns to be filled. Good parents try to model the unconditional love of God yet fall short bringing additional pain, hurt and feelings of abandonment. Great earthly parents can fill some of the void in your heart however it is only Abba, Daddy, Father God which gives HIS unconditional love and fills your heart's deepest desire to be loved.

"[4] But when the right time came, God sent his Son, born of a woman, subject to the law. [5] God sent him to buy freedom for us who were slaves to the law, so that he could **adopt us as his very own children**. [6] And because we are his children, God has sent the **Spirit of his Son into our hearts**, prompting us to call out, "Abba, Father." [7] Now you are no longer a slave but God's own child. And **since you are his child,** God has made you his heir."

-   *Galatians 4:4-7*

God's love paid for your freedom from the curse of the law so that you can be restored as a child of God.

The Spirit of sonship fills the void in your heart. The craving to be loved which is deep in your heart has been satisfied by your adoption into your Father's household. You have been adopted by the King. You are no longer a slave. You are an heir of God with all HIS INHERITANCE waiting for you. He calls you his friend. He wants you to spend time with him in his presence. He has accepted you just as you are. The void in your heart is filled.

You are a son or daughter of Abba, Daddy, Father God and are no longer an orphan. The Spirit of Adoption which is HIS unconditional love for you as HIS child has filled the longing desire in your heart.

The cure to the Orphan's lonely Spirit is to receive Daddy's love.

Your DADDY LOVES you!

Receive your adoption papers and celebrate the good news!

Jesus Christ legally and judicially restored you back to your legal family as a Child of God in the image and likeness of God. You have all the legal rights and privileges as a son or daughter of God. You are BLESSED. You have life abundantly. You have the mind of Christ and the Wisdom of God living in you.

20

Righteous

"Fraud" Day 20

First published October 18, 2018 in the Fraud Series – The Repple Minute

Day 20 of the Fraud committed by Satan against man

Righteous

Adam trusted and believed the deception and fraudulent ways of Satan thus man lost their right standing with God (Righteousness) in the Garden of Eden.

Before you were born again and redeemed, you were born into the power of darkness. It is your ancestors' (Adam and Eve) disobedience which caused you to be born with a self-centered selfish nature. Before you were saved, did a single righteous act make you righteous? If you performed many righteous acts did it make you righteous? No, you were still a sinner living in darkness under Satan's rule.

Before being born again, as a sinner there are no number of righteous acts which can make you righteous.

For since [it was] through a man that death [came into the world, it is] also through a Man that the resurrection of the dead [has come]. 1 Corinthians 15:21

> "²¹For He made Him who knew no sin *to be* sin for us, that we might become the **righteousness** of God in Him."
> -   *2 Corinthians 5:21 NKJV*

God has demonstrated HIS AGAPE love for all mankind through giving HIS one and only Son to die for ALL sin once and for ALL. There is no sin which Jesus did not die for on the cross. There is no sin which He did not forgive.

Now as a born again, redeemed follower of Jesus Christ, it is also true because of what Christ Jesus did for all mankind there is no sin or amount of sin which will cause you to become a sinner again. You have been made righteous by the Lamb of God Jesus Christ. If Jesus' death was not for all sin, HIS death and resurrection would not be complete. HE died for all sin.

This is not a license to sin; this is victory over sin and death. You have the righteousness of Christ in you. You are in Christ Jesus sitting at the right hand of God the father. Your righteousness is in Christ.

You have moved from the bondage of being a sinner (old nature) into the righteousness of Christ Jesus (new nature). Your identity/nature is in Christ Jesus completely forgiven and redeemed. You are the Righteousness of God in Christ Jesus. You are no longer under condemnation for those who live according to the Spirit.

You have been made righteous in Christ Jesus through HIS death and resurrection.

Your sins are no longer counted against you. God will remember them no more.

Your sins are forgiven, removed and forgotten as far as the east is from the west.

Your sins and unrighteous acts of lying, anger, hatred, unforgiveness, neglect, drunkenness, rebellion, disbelief, hard heart, disobedience, deceitfulness, manipulation, sexual sins, immorality, abortion, selfishness, lust, craving, boasting, and idol worship of this world have been washed clean by the blood of the sacrificial LAMB Jesus Christ.

Jesus Christ legally and judicially restored you back to your legal family as a Child of God in the image and likeness of God. You have all the legal rights and privileges as a son or daughter of God. You are BLESSED. You have life abundantly. You have the mind of Christ and the Wisdom of God living in you.

21

Transformed Life

"Fraud" Day 21

First published October 19, 2018 in the Fraud Series – The Repple Minute

Day 21 of the Fraud committed by Satan against man

Transformed Life

We are made in God's image and likeness of AGAPE Love. This was lost at the Fall through Adam. Selfishness, self-desire, self-consciousness, and disbelief of God entered the world. We are born believing the lies of the Prince of this world Satan.

We have been trained by Satan's world's system not the Kingdom of God system.

Don't copy the behavior and customs of this world, but let **God transform you** into a new person by changing the way you think. Then you will learn to know God's will for you, which is good and pleasing and perfect.
- Romans 12:2 NLT

What is a transformed life?

- A born-again life is a transformed life sealed with the Holy Spirit living in them.

- A life transformed no longer believes the lies, behaviors and customs of this world but trusts God's Word being revealed to them through the Holy Spirit.

- The transformed life has been freed from the poverty mindset in bondage and slavery to the world's cursed system of painful toil and sweat.

- The transformed life is a NEW BORN-AGAIN LIFE in CHRIST JESUS.

- The transformed life is receiving and growing in All the Love of God.

- The transformed life is entering your NEW FAMILY which God designed for you from the beginning of time.

- The transformed life is being transformed, recreated, restored, redeemed and born again into the image and likeness of God. Which is LOVE.

- The transformed life is changing the way you think recognizing your New Identity, New Creation, New Family in Christ Jesus. The old selfish nature was hung on the cross.

- The transformed life is bringing HEAVEN to earth now with the HOLY SPRIT living in you now.

- The transformed life is knowing God and HIS will for you to be transformed back into HIS image to LOVE others.

- The transformed life knows they are a son and daughter of God.

- The transformed life knows they have been redeemed and made the Righteousness of God in Christ Jesus. They can enter God's presence knowing God sees them through the blood of Jesus.

God's will is good, pleasing, and perfect. HIS love is living in the transformed life. God's will is that ALL would be transformed not religious but be transformed into HIS CHRIST-LIKENESS of LOVE.

Jesus Christ legally and judicially restored you back to your legal family as a Child of God in the image and likeness of God. You have all the legal rights and privileges as a son or daughter of God. You are BLESSED.

You have life abundantly. You have the mind of Christ and the Wisdom of God living in you.

God loves you. HE is love. Trust the TRUTH of HIS LOVE living in you today.

22

Eternal Life

"Fraud" Day 22

First published October 22, 2018 in the Fraud Series – The Repple Minute

Day 22 of the Fraud committed by Satan against man

Eternal Life

We are made in God's image and likeness as Eternal Spirit beings filled with God's DIVINE Love. Temporal life (spiritual death) is from Satan taken stolen from Adam. Jesus Christ redeemed us from the temporal and has given us ETERNAL LIFE in HIM NOW.

Eternal life is not something which is **credited** to you when you die.

- Eternal life is something **you <u>become</u> now**.
- Eternal life is in Christ Jesus your new being now.
- Eternal life is your New Creation now.

- Eternal life was/is imputed to you on the cross now.
- Eternal life is NOW.
- Eternal life is imputed to you through the Divine exchange of the New Creation now in Christ Jesus.
- Eternal life is in your born-again LIFE in the SPIRIT of God entering into you through the Holy Spirit NOW.
- Eternal Life is the Spirit of God living in you now. Your body is the tabernacle carrying the Holy Spirit which is the Divine Nature of God living in you now.

"Therefore, if anyone is in Christ, the **new creation has come**: The **old has gone**, the **new is here**!" *2 Corinthians 5:17 NIV*

"This means that anyone who belongs to Christ has **become a new person**. The **old life** is gone; a **new life** has begun!" *2 Corinthians 5:17 NLT*

The sin of all mankind was imputed to Jesus and HIS RIGHTOUSNESS was imputed to all who receive HIS GIFT of LIFE (Eternal) and RIGHTEOUSNESS.

Fact is that life is in Jesus Christ through the Holy Spirit, not in your temporal five senses. The glorious day of heaven begins now with the removal of sin consciousness and the imputation of righteousness consciousness in your NEW CREATION of the Holy Spirit.

What you confess you will possess.

- Confess with your mouth that you are a NEW CREATION made in the image and likeness of God.
- Confess with your mouth that Jesus is Lord and the HOLY SPIRIT lives in you.
- Confess with your mouth that "I am the Righteousness of God in Christ Jesus."
- Confess with your mouth that the divine nature of God is living in me through the Holy Spirit.
- Confess with your mouth that God's love is living in me and that HIS AGAPE LOVE in me is greater than any circumstance or problem which can come at me today.
- Confess with your mouth that I was crucified with Christ, I died with Christ, I was raised with Christ and I sit at God's right hand now in Christ Jesus.
- Confess with your mouth that I have been redeemed by the blood of Jesus and washed clean of all sin past, present and future. I can enter into God's presence NOW because of Jesus Christ and the Holy Spirit living in me.

Heaven is now in a state of LIFE ETERNAL in the Holy Spirit not something which is credited to you later. Eternity begins now in Christ Jesus.

Jesus Christ legally and judicially restored you back to your legal family as a Child of God in the image and likeness of God. You have all the legal rights and privileges as a son or daughter of God. You are BLESSED. You have life abundantly. You have the mind of Christ and the Wisdom of God living in you.

23

Victory over death

"Fraud" Day 23

First published October 23, 2018 in the Fraud Series – The Repple Minute

Day 23 of the Fraud committed by Satan against man

Victory over death

Satan's fraud in the Garden of Eden caused man to die both physically and spiritually. Death was not God's plan for man. God designed man to live forever.

The Devil wants you to believe that you have not died, that death is still in the future. No, no, no, no! The devil is stealing the victory Jesus' death gives to ALL. Jesus' Sacrificial Death was given freely on the cross by the payment of Jesus' blood for all to have victory over death, sin, curse and judgment **now**. What Jesus did in the past is for ALL to receive life and freedom now.

Your life begins at Jesus' death – "Christ Crucified." You are a Spirit Being created in God's image from the beginning for HIS PURPOSE. Your life has been crucified "died with Christ," just like Paul says boldly about his death and life in Christ. Paul is writing about his new life.

Here are three different translations for the same passage. Then you can put your name in a paraphrased passage.

"**20** I have been **crucified with Christ** [that is, in Him I have shared His crucifixion]; it is no longer I who live, but **Christ lives in me**. The *life* I now live in the body I live by faith [by adhering to, relying on, and completely trusting] in the Son of God, who loved me and gave Himself up for me."
- *Galatians 2:20 AMP*

"As far as the Law is concerned I may consider that **I died on the cross with Christ**. And my present life is not that of the old "I", but **the living Christ within me**. The bodily life I now live, I live believing in the Son of God, who loved me and sacrificed himself for me. Consequently I refuse to stultify the grace of God by reverting to the Law. For if righteousness were possible under the Law then Christ died for nothing!"
- *Galatians 2:20-21 JB Phillips*

"**19-21** What actually took place is this: I tried keeping rules and working my head off to please God, and it didn't work. So I quit being a "law man" so that I could be *God's* man. Christ's life showed me how, and enabled me to do it. I identified myself completely with him. Indeed, **I have been crucified with Christ**. My ego is no longer central. It is no longer important that I appear righteous before you or have your good opinion, and I am no longer driven to impress God. **Christ lives in me**. The life you see me living is not "mine," but it is lived by faith in the Son of God, who loved me and gave himself for me. I am not going to go back on that."
- *Galatians 2:19-21 Message*

Put your name in the following paraphrase of Galatians 2:20. Speak it out loud!

"I _____ have died with Christ. I _____ have been Crucified with Christ on the Cross and it is no longer _____ who lives but Christ living in me. I am a living Spirit Being designed to live forever in Christ Jesus."

You have died already and are alive in the power of the Holy Spirit housed in your Sanctified, Holy Temple through the cleansing power of the Blood of Jesus Christ.

Jesus Christ legally and judicially restored you back to your legal family as a Child of God in the image and likeness of God. You have all the legal rights and privileges as a son or daughter of God. You are BLESSED. You have life abundantly. You have the mind of Christ and the Wisdom of God living in you.

24

Security Day

"Fraud" Day 24

First published October 24, 2018 in the Fraud Series – The Repple Minute

Day 24 of the Fraud committed by Satan against man

Security

Merriam-Webster defines fraud as follows: intentional perversion of truth in order to induce another to part with something of value or to surrender a legal right.

Fraud was committed in the Garden of Eden when Satan deceived Adam to give up his security in God. Now, man seeks security from their work, government, relationships, wealth and position. Man has a legal right to have their security restored.

"Whoever **dwells** in the **shelter** of the Most High will **rest** in the shadow of the Almighty."
- *Psalms 91:1*

Psalms 91:1 tells us we get security and protection by **dwelling** in the **shelter** of the Lord. It is like Noah and his family sealed and protected in the Ark. The storms and raging seas crashed all around the Ark yet they were safe in the dwelling place of the Most High God in HIS PROTECTION. You are sealed and protected in your salvation by the blood of Jesus on the cross.

The peace and protection the world tries to give is through the temporal. However, the **rest** and peace which comes through **dwelling** - abiding in Christ Jesus - brings an eternal peace which passes all understanding.

Dwelling in the shelter of the Most High is receiving God's love which was demonstrated on the Cross through the blood of Jesus Christ to justify all mankind so that you can be called a Child of God and enter into HIS PRESENCE. This is entering into rest in the shadow of the Almighty, knowing, trusting, and receiving God's love in Christ Jesus' finished work on the cross, knowing you have been made righteous, holy and sanctified by the blood of Jesus Christ. You are washed clean. God sees you as if you have never sinned.

Financial Peace and protection is not the same as the **rest** in the shadow of the Almighty's Peace.

> "**27** Peace I leave with you; My [perfect] peace I give to you; not as the world gives do I give to you. Do not let your heart be troubled, nor let it be afraid. [Let My perfect peace calm you in every circumstance and give you courage and strength for every challenge.]"
> - *John 14:27 AMP*

> "Whoever **dwells** in the **shelter** of the Most High will **rest** in the shadow of the Almighty."
> - *Psalm 91:1*

Dwell means to abide, inhabit, live, marry, occupy, reside, sit down, settle, stay and rule. Where you are dwelling with your mind, your will and emotions will determine your security and protection.

Dwelling in God's perfect love which is living in you through the Holy Spirit will allow you to **rest** in the shadow of the Almighty.

Security and protection is only in Jesus the Anointed One.

Receive HIS love, dwell in HIS Shelter and receive HIS ETERNAL REST now in Jesus' Name.

Jesus Christ legally and judicially restored you back to your legal family as a Child of God in the image and likeness of God. You have all the legal rights and privileges as a son or daughter of God. You are BLESSED. You have life abundantly. You have the mind of Christ and the Wisdom of God living in you.

25

Right to be a Child of God

"Fraud" Day 25

First published October 25, 2018 in the Fraud Series – The Repple Minute

Day 25 of the Fraud committed by Satan against man

Right to be a Child of God

Merriam-Webster defines fraud as follows: intentional perversion of truth in order to induce another to part with something of value or to surrender a legal right.

Adam surrender man's legal right to be a child of God to Satan in the Garden of Eden.

> "**12** But to as many as did receive *and* welcome Him, He **gave the right** [the authority, the privilege] to **become children of God**, *that is*, to those who believe in (adhere to, trust in, and rely on) His name."
> - *John 1:12 AMP*

The Greek word for "right" is exousia which means power to act, authority. It comes from the root word of exesti which means it is permitted, lawful.

So what is your legal, lawful right?

Yes, you have the authority and legal right to become children of God!

Recognize that the right is not earned, it is **given**!

How do you exercise this right to become a child of God? Read John 1:12 again to get the answer.

> "**12** But to as many as did **receive** *and* **welcome** Him, He **gave the right** [the authority, the privilege] to become children of God, *that is*, to those who **believe** in (**adhere** to, **trust in**, and **rely on**) His name"
> *John 1:12 AMP*

So, you exercise your right by the following:

- Receiving
- Welcoming
- Believing
- Adhering
- Trusting
- Relying

The name of Jesus is above every name. You are exercising your right to receive your pardon from the curse, judgment, condemnation, sickness, disease, shame, sin and guilt. Your payment was/is made in the name of Jesus through HIS BLOOD on the Cross.

You can receive your "Right and Privileges" in Jesus' Name by trusting in the finished, complete work of God's amazing love on the Cross to redeem mankind from the fall. God reconciled mankind to be in RIGHTEOUS standing before God just as if you/we had never sinned.

Which "right" are you receiving, and which is greater? Your "right" in Jesus' name given to you to become a child of God or your earthly human rights? Are you fighting for your rights here on earth or are you defending the NAME of JESUS who has given you the "Right" through HIS Blood to be a child of God?

Receive your "right" in Jesus' name.

Jesus Christ legally and judicially restored you back to your legal family as a Child of God in the image and likeness of God. You have all the legal rights and privileges as a son or daughter of God. You are BLESSED. You have life abundantly. You have the mind of Christ and the Wisdom of God living in you.

26

New Creation Life is now!

"Fraud" Day 26

First published October 26, 2018 in the Fraud Series — The Repple Minute

Day 26 of the Fraud committed by Satan against man

New Creation Life is **now!**

Satan committed fraud in the Garden of Eden causing death. Yet Christ came to bring Life.

> "Therefore, if anyone is in Christ, the **new creation** has come: The old has gone, the new is here!"
> - *2 Corinthians 5:17*

Death is behind you and the New Creation Resurrected Life is **now!** Death was taken and nailed to the Cross. You are **in Christ**. Christ died as you. HE arose as you. You are the **New Creation in Christ now** and will never die again

[8] Now **if we have <u>died with Christ</u>**, we believe that **we will also <u>live</u> [together] <u>with Him</u>**, [9] because we know [the self-evident truth] that Christ, having been raised from the dead, **<u>will never die again</u>**; death no longer has power over Him. [10] For the death that He died, He died to sin [ending its power and paying the sinner's debt] once and for all; and the life that He lives, He lives to [glorify] God [in unbroken fellowship with Him]. [11] Even so, consider yourselves to be dead to sin [and your relationship to it broken], but alive to God [in unbroken fellowship with Him] **in Christ Jesus.**
- *Romans 6:8-11 AMP*

- When do you experience victory - **now** or in heaven?

- When do you overcome - **now** or in heaven?

- When are you reconciled to God - **now** or in heaven?

- When do you have peace with God - **now** or in heaven?

- When do you get rest - **now** or in heaven?

- When are you more than a conqueror - **now** or in heaven?

- When can you do all things through Christ who strengthens you - **now** or in heaven?

- When are you restored into the image of God - **now** or in heaven?

- When do you receive there is no condemnation - **now** or in heaven?

- When do you receive no more sin, guilt, shame or inferior complex - **now** or in heaven?

- When do you become a saint - **now** or in heaven?

- When do you become a King and Priest - **now** or in heaven?

- When do you receive Shalom Peace - **now** or in heaven?

- When do you become partakers of God's Divine Nature - **now** or in heaven?

- When are you judged and declared RIGHTEOUS - **now** or in heaven?

- When are all sins forgiven - **now** or in heaven?

- When are all sins removed - **now** or in heaven?

- When was sickness and disease removed - **now** or in heaven?

- When do you die in Christ - **now** or in heaven?

- When do you receive the resurrection power of Christ - **now** or in heaven?

- When does the Holy Spirit, Christ Jesus dwell in you - **now** or in heaven?

- When are you redeemed - **now** or in heaven?

- When does your born-again life begin - **now** or in heaven?

- When does the power, love and sound mind of Christ come into you - **now** or in heaven?

- When do you receive and put on the Robe of Righteousness - **now** or in heaven?

- When are you in Christ - **now** or in heaven?

- When do you sit on the Throne in Christ - **now** or in heaven?

- When are you judged for your sin - **now** or in heaven?

- When is the curse removed - **now** or in heaven?

- When do you receive eternal life - **now** or in heaven?

- When are you made Righteous, Holy and Sanctified - **now** or in heaven?

- When do you receive the Gift of Righteousness - **now** or in heaven?

- When do you conquer death - **now** or in heaven?

- When do you become a new creation - **now** or in heaven?

Death is behind you, not in front of you. You have already died in Christ as a believer in the Resurrected Christ Jesus. You will never die because you have already died with Christ and are living now in Christ. Ask the Holy Spirit to reveal this to you. Death is not ahead of you.

Jesus Christ legally and judicially restored you back to your legal family as a Child of God in the image and likeness of God. You have all the legal rights and privileges as a son or daughter of God. You are BLESSED. You have life abundantly. You have the mind of Christ and the Wisdom of God living in you.

27

Who are you?

"Fraud" Day 27

First published October 29, 2018 in the Fraud Series – The Repple Minute

Day 27 of the Fraud committed by Satan against man

Who are you?

Merriam-Webster defines fraud as follows: intentional perversion of truth in order to induce another to part with something of value or to surrender a legal right.

Satan stole man's identity in the Garden of Eden.

Where do you get your identity through your work? Your success? Your wealth? Your friendships? Your church? Your power or position? Your recognition in the community? Your family? Your spouse? Your children? Your hobbies?

"**21** For He made Him who knew no sin *to be* sin for us, that **we might become the righteousness of God in Him.**"
- *2 Corinthians 5:21 NKJV*

You are the Righteousness of God in HIM Christ Jesus the Anointed One.

When your identity is in Christ, you are a **child** of God. You are a **Son/Daughter** of God and Jesus calls you **friend**.

"**26** For you [who are born-again have been reborn from above—spiritually transformed, renewed, sanctified and] are all **children of God** [set apart for His purpose with full rights and privileges] through faith in Christ Jesus."
- *Galatians 3:26 AMP*

"The Spirit himself testifies with our spirit that we are **God's children**. Now if we are children, then we are heirs—heirs of God and co-heirs with Christ, if indeed we share in his sufferings in order that we may also share in his glory."
- *Romans 8:16-17 NIV*

"Because you are sons, God sent the Spirit of his Son into our hearts, the Spirit who calls out, "Abba, Father." So you are no longer a slave, but a son; and since you are a son, God has made you also an heir."
- *Galatians 4:6-7 BSB*

"¹² My command is this: Love each other as I have loved you. ¹³ Greater love has no one than this: to lay down one's life for one's friends. ¹⁴ You are my friends if you do what I command. ¹⁵ I no longer call you servants, because a servant does not know his master's business. Instead, I have called you friends, for everything that I learned from my Father I have made known to you."
- *John 15:12-15 NIV*

As a child, son and friend of God, the grace and favor of God is with you in the pit, prison and palace. Walk today in God's favor as a Son and Daughter of the King of Kings and Lord of Lords. You are an heir to all God has and owns. HIS inheritance is yours. Your identity is in Christ Jesus as a Son and Daughter of God.

You have God's Devine Nature living in you. HIS SEED of the Word of God is alive and active in you. Everything you need has been provided for you through Jesus Christ.

Jesus Christ legally and judicially restored you back to your legal family as a Child of God in the image and likeness of God. You have all the legal rights and privileges as a son or daughter of God. You are BLESSED. You have life abundantly. You have the mind of Christ and the Wisdom of God living in you.

28

Agent of Redemption

"Fraud" Day 28

First published October 30, 2018 in the Fraud Series – The Repple Minute

Day 28 of the Fraud committed by Satan against man

Being an Agent of Redemption

Merriam-Webster defines fraud as follows: intentional perversion of truth in order to induce another to part with something of value or to surrender a legal right.

Adam believed the perversion of truth caused by the lies of Satan and allowed death, sin, sickness, disease, selfishness, revenge, hate, bitterness, injustice, bitterness, lack, fear, worry, depression, condemnation, oppression, blame, shame, guilt and the satanic rule of earth.

"¹⁷ For if, by the trespass of the one man **Adam**, death reigned through that one man **Adam**, how much more will those who receive God's abundant provision of grace and of the gift of righteousness reign in life through the one man, **Jesus Christ**!"
- (*Romans 5:17 NIV with my emphasis in bold*).

One man Adam believed Satan which caused destruction and One man Jesus Christ the Anointed One brought redemption to all that receive the gift of righteousness (right Standing with God).

- I am redeemed from eternal death and given eternal life by the resurrected Christ Jesus living in me now.

- I am redeemed from the curse by the Blood of Jesus revealed through the Holy Spirit.

- I am redeemed from the work cursed system of pain, toil and sweat of the brow through Christ Jesus.

- I am redeemed from the curse of sickness and disease by the Blood of Jesus Christ.

- I am redeemed from all sin and all the consequences of sin - shame, guilt, condemnation, oppression, depression, injustice, unforgiveness, orphan spirit, rejection, fear, and lack by the resurrected Christ Jesus.

So, what is the purpose of redemption?

"21 God made him who had no sin to be sin or us, so that in him we might become the righteousness of God."
- *2Corinthians 5:21 NIV*

The purpose of redemption was to bring mankind back into relationship with God so Jesus took all sin, sickness, and disease caused by the fall and we received HIS RIGHTEOUSNESS through Jesus Christ.

You are a New Creation in Christ Jesus. You have been redeemed, restored and reconciled to God in Christ Jesus. Jesus took all sin, spiritual death, judgment, wickedness and the curse on the cross. HE restored followers of Christ into their rightful position sitting at the right hand of God in Christ Jesus. HE took mankind's wickedness and gave mankind HIS RIGHTEOUNESS.

Everything you do can be Redemptive. You are an agent of redemption and reconciliation bringing everything in line with the Purpose of God. The will of God is that "All mankind" would receive the love of God through Jesus Christ's shed blood poured out for all mankind to redeem mankind from the fall and high treason of Adam.

You are an agent/ambassador on assignment to bring Redemption.

Your work is redemptive.

Your service is redemptive.

Your family is redemptive.

Your health is redemptive.

Your finances are redemptive.

Your children are redemptive.

Your marriage is redemptive.

Your life is redemptive.

Your wealth and money are redemptive.

Your community, state and country are redemptive.

Everything you do today can have a redemptive purpose.

Jesus Christ legally and judicially restored you back to your legal family as a Child of God in the image and likeness of God. You have all the legal rights and privileges as a son or daughter of God. You are BLESSED. You have life abundantly. You have the mind of Christ and the Wisdom of God living in you.

29

Lack of Knowledge Destroys

"Fraud" Day 29

First published October 31, 2018 in the Fraud Series – The Repple Minute

Day 29 of the Fraud committed by Satan against man

Lack of Knowledge Destroys

Merriam-Webster defines fraud as follows: intentional perversion of truth in order to induce another to part with something of value or to surrender a legal right.

Adam surrendered man's legal right of dominion over all the earth to Satan in the Garden of Eden.

> "My people are destroyed for a lack of knowledge."
> - *Hosea 4:6*

What kind of knowledge causes "My People" to perish? **Unbelief** is a belief in self more than God: My power, my knowledge, my strength, my intellect is greater than God's. This is the path to destruction. Wide and broad is the road to destruction but narrow is the path which leads to the knowledge of Christ's redemption. **Faith** is believing in God more than self.

The Israelites came to a point where they did not want God's Word to get in the way of their belief/legal system. What they believed, and their intellectual knowledge of man, traditions and doctrine they thought was greater than the Wisdom of God's Word.

1. The lack of knowledge of God's Redemption Plan is unbelief in Christ's complete finished work on the cross, which will lead His people to perish and lead to destruction.

2. The lack of knowledge about being written into God's inheritance as an heir of God and joint heir with Jesus Christ will lead "My people to be destroyed for a lack of HIS KNOWLEDGE."

3. Lack of knowledge on the authority HIS Children have over the enemy, death, sickness and sin will cause "My people to perish and be destroyed."

4. The lack of knowledge about God's AGAPE love will cause HIS people to live in fear, condemnation, lack, shame, guilt, unforgiveness, bitterness, and blame so that they will not experience the joy, freedom, peace, rest, power and victory of the Cross. "My people will be destroyed because they lack HIS KNOWLEDGE of love."

5. The lack of knowledge about God's Grace will cause "my people to perish and be destroyed because they want to perform and earn God's AGAPE love." It is Christ's performance and demonstration of HIS sacrificial love on the cross which redeemed mankind, not your effort. Thinking you can earn God's AGAPE love through your efforts destroys "my people."

6. The lack of knowledge about your identity in Christ as the Righteousness of God in Christ Jesus will cause my people to perish and be destroyed.

7. The lack of knowledge about God's Sabbath Rest of provision, prosperity and abundance for HIS CHILDREN causes them to live in the work cursed system of the world of painful toil and sweat.

For the message of the cross is foolishness to those who are perishing, but to us who are being saved it is the power of God. For it is written: "I will destroy the wisdom of the wise; the intelligence of the intelligent I will frustrate."

Where is the wise person? Where is the teacher of the law? Where is the philosopher of this age? Has not God made foolish the wisdom of the world?

For since in the wisdom of God the world through its wisdom did not know him, God was pleased through the foolishness of what was preached to save those who believe. Jews demand signs and Greeks look for wisdom, but we preach Christ crucified: a stumbling block to Jews and foolishness to Gentiles, but to those whom God has called, both Jews and Greeks, Christ the power of God and the wisdom of God. For the foolishness of God is wiser than human wisdom, and the weakness of God is stronger than human strength.

Therefore, as it is written:

> "Let the one who boasts boast in the Lord."
> *(1 Corinthians 1:18-25, 31 NIV)*

Jesus Christ legally and judicially restored you back to your legal family as a Child of God in the image and likeness of God. You have all the legal rights and privileges as a son or daughter of God. You are BLESSED. You have life abundantly. You have the mind of Christ and the Wisdom of God living in you.

30

Freedom

"Fraud" Day 30

First published November 1, 2018 in the Fraud Series – The Repple Minute

Day 30 of the Fraud committed by Satan against man

Freedom

Merriam-Webster defines fraud as follows: intentional perversion of truth in order to induce another to part with something of value or to surrender a legal right.

Adam surrendered man's legal right of freedom in the Garden of Eden.

Freedom is God's idea.

"The LORD God took the man and put him in the Garden of Eden to work it and take care of it. [16] And the LORD God commanded the man, "You are **free** to eat from any tree in the garden; [17] but you must not eat from the tree of the knowledge of good and evil, for when you eat of it you will surely die.""
- *Genesis 2:15*

God gave man freedom with boundaries. Because we were created in God's image and out of His great AGAPE love, the boundaries that God places for us are always for our own good, as well as the good of His creation.

There are consequences when you go outside of God's purpose and will. Adam and Eve violated / disobeyed the creative purpose which God intended for mankind. God's purpose for mankind was for us to eat in total freedom in the abundance of the Garden of Eden, and experience the full presence of God.

The Garden of Eden represents perfection in which man lived without sin, sickness and death. It was devoid of sin, and it was here that Adam and Eve were able to communicate perfectly with God without the separation of sin.

Adam and Eve fell to the temptation of disbelief and listened to Satan. They doubted God's Word. They went outside the boundary of God's Word and lost their freedom to eat in abundance from the Garden of Eden, and most importantly, their fellowship with God.

The good news is that Jesus Christ has restored and reconciled us in HIS ABUNDANCE. HE defeated Satan on the Cross and has given mankind victory over the power of sin, lack, sickness and death. HE has exchanged HIS righteousness for your sin of disobedience, self-reliance, selfishness and pride. You have the Holy Spirit living in you now.

God has known you from the beginning of creation. HE shaped and molded you in your mother's womb. HE has a creative purpose for you. HE wants to live, reign and rule in you through the Holy Spirit. HE wants your total trust, obedience and attention. HE wants you to have no other gods before HIM. HE wants all of your heart, mind, soul and strength. HE has restored you, forgiven you, and reconciled you in Christ Jesus. HE exchanged your sin for HIS righteousness in Christ Jesus.

> "So if the Son sets you free, you will be free indeed."
> *John 8:36*

Your freedom is in Jesus Christ. HE has set you free. Freedom and victory is God's plan for your life.

Jesus Christ legally and judicially restored you back to your legal family as a Child of God in the image and likeness of God. You have all the legal rights and privileges as a son or daughter of God. You are BLESSED. You have life abundantly. You have the mind of Christ and the Wisdom of God living in you.

31

Justice through the Court

"Fraud" Day 31

First published November 2, 2018 in the Fraud Series – The Repple Minute

Day 31 of the Fraud committed by Satan against man

Justice through the Court

Merriam-Webster defines fraud as follows: intentional perversion of truth in order to induce another to part with something of value or to surrender a legal right.

Adam surrendered man's legal right to Justice to Satan rule of this world in the Garden of Eden.

Can you get justice through the court systems of this world?

You can get a monetary award of money or get someone sentenced. You may win and get what you desire. This would be called justice in this world. This is not the same justice which Jesus Christ gives you.

Man's justice is always temporal while God's Justice is eternal and lasting. If you are seeking justice in this world, you will not find it. It only comes through Jesus Christ. The court systems may award you what you want but they cannot give you peace and contentment. The world promises that the pursuit of pleasures and riches of this world will satisfy;

> "⁹ But people who long to be rich fall into temptation and are trapped by many foolish and harmful desires that plunge them into **ruin and destruction.** ¹⁰ For the **love** of money is the root of all kinds of evil. And some people, **craving money,** have wandered from the true faith and **pierced themselves with many sorrows.**"
> -   *1 Timothy 6:9-11 NIV*

We are no longer slaves to the justice of this world. We are sons and daughters of God receiving Freedom and Justice through Jesus Christ.

Justice comes only with the blood of Jesus Christ which redeemed us from the slavery to this world cursed system. It is only through Jesus Christ do you get justice.

> "With his own blood--not the blood of goats and calves--he entered the Most Holy Place once for all time and **secured our redemption <u>forever</u>.**"
> - *Hebrews 9:12 NLT*

Justice in this worlds system means money. Justice in the Kingdom of God is being released from the bondage and destruction of sin, lack and sickness and disease. Money can be a false god. Money promises false safety, security, false happiness and false hope. Money cannot buy the forgiveness of your sins and the healing of your diseases. Money cannot purchase the peace of God which transcends all understanding.

> "² Bless the LORD, O my soul, and forget not all his benefits: ³ Who **forgiveth all thine iniquities**; **who healeth all thy diseases**;"
> - *Psalm 103*

> "And the peace of God, which transcends all understanding, will guard your hearts and your minds in Christ Jesus."
> - *Philippians 4:7 NIV*

Jesus Christ paid the payment for JUSTICE. God's love for all mankind redeemed man from the fallen condition of sin and depravity in Christ Jesus on the cross. Jesus' blood paid for all unjust acts, accidents, and words spoken over you. Jesus broke the **curse of injustice and brings HIS JUSTICE**. You are JUST (RIGHTEOUS) because of what Jesus did. You are in a fallen and depraved condition because of what your ancestors Adam and Eve did. God has given you free will to choose life or death. **Life** is in Christ Jesus, the **just,** or **death** in Adam and Eve, **injustice**.

Jesus Christ legally and judicially restored you back to your legal family as a Child of God in the image and likeness of God. You have all the legal rights and privileges as a son or daughter of God. You are BLESSED. You have life abundantly. You have the mind of Christ and the Wisdom of God living in you.

32

God's Glory

"Fraud" Day 32

First published November 5, 2018 in the Fraud Series – The Repple Minute

Day 32 of the Fraud committed by Satan against man

God's Glory

Merriam-Webster defines fraud as follows: intentional perversion of truth in order to induce another to part with something of value or to surrender a legal right.

Adam surrendered man's legal right of God's Glory to Satan in the Garden of Eden.

God's Glory is His Agape Love, His Presence, His Power and His Goodness.

When you squeeze an orange, orange juice comes out. When you squeeze a lemon, lemon juice come out. When you squeeze a follower of Christ, "Jesus Juice" comes out.

God's Agape Love, Presence, Power and Goodness in you produces Jesus Juice.

> "22 But the fruit of the [Holy] Spirit [the work which **His presence within accomplishes**] is (AGAPE) love, joy (gladness), peace, patience (an even temper, forbearance), kindness, goodness (benevolence), faithfulness,
>
> 23 Gentleness (meekness, humility), self-control (self-restraint, continence). **Against such things there is no law [that can bring a charge].**" *Galatians 5:22-23 AMP*

The Holy Spirit produces Jesus Juice which is one fruit producing all the following:

- AGAPE Love

- Joy

- Peace

- Patience

- Kindness

- Goodness

- Faithfulness

- Gentleness

- Self-Control

HIS presence in you produces the Jesus Juice, not your effort. HIS Holy Spirit working through you - the branch, the pipe, the water hose - produces the Jesus Juice. When you work, HE rests. When you rest HE WORKS.

Your stressing does not produce Jesus Juice. Your fear and anxiety do not produce Jesus Juice. You beating up on yourself with condemnation, guilt, lack and shame does not produce Jesus Juice.

You have been freed from all oppression, condemnation, guilt and the law which judges man. Jesus took all the law of the knowledge of good and evil on the cross and has given you LIFE.

The charges against you have been dropped.

God's AGAPE love for you defeated fear. God's AGAPE love for you was demonstrated on the cross for you. Receive HIS AGAPE love today knowing Jesus took all the wrath against you and has given you HIS RIGHTEOUSNESS. The charges have been dropped against you.

This is not too-good-to-be-true. It is the original Good News. Receive God's unconditional AGAPE love. You are no longer a slave to lack, stress, anxiety, worry, fear, oppression and condemnation. This was nailed on the Cross in Christ Jesus.

Jesus Christ legally and judicially restored you back to your legal family as a Child of God in the image and likeness of God. You have all the legal rights and privileges as a son or daughter of God. You are BLESSED. You have life abundantly. You have the mind of Christ and the Wisdom of God living in you.

33

Power of WORDS

"Fraud" Day 33

First published November 6, 2018 in the Fraud Series – The Repple Minute

Day 33 of the Fraud committed by Satan against man

Power of WORDS

Merriam-Webster defines fraud as follows: intentional perversion of truth in order to induce another to part with something of value or to surrender a legal right.

Adam surrendered man's legal right of God's Power of Words to Satan in the Garden of Eden. Your words can create life or death.

> "Death and life are in the power of the tongue, And those who love it and indulge it will eat its fruit and bear the consequences of their words."
> - *Proverbs 18:21 Amplified Bible (AMP).*

God spoke creation into existence. There is power in words. God **said**, "let there be." God's word is outside of time; it is eternal. God's Word is alive now, today and continually.

The Word is living, active and power.

> "For the **word of God is living and active _and_ full of power** [making it operative, energizing, and effective]. It is sharper than any two-edged sword, penetrating as far as the division of the soul and spirit [the completeness of a person], and of both joints and marrow [the deepest parts of our nature], exposing _and_ judging the very thoughts and intentions of the heart."
> - _Hebrews 4:12_

God's word is living now.

God's word is active now.

God's word is full of power now.

The resurrected power of Christ is living in you through the Holy Spirit. The Word of God is living in you. The Temple of the Holy Spirit resides in you through the Holy Spirit.

Speak the Word of God over yourself, your circumstance and your problem.

You have power over the defeated foe, the prince of this world, Satan. You have been redeemed from the curse of the law. Poverty, sickness, disease and death are part of the curse (read the curses in Deuteronomy 28).

You have been given Authority, Power and Dominion over the works of the enemy. Sin, sickness and disease are works of the devil which came at the fall. Speak to fear, "fear get out of here". "Sickness be removed now in Jesus name".

Jesus' body was beaten and bruised for our healing.

Salvation and healing is all part of the Atonement and New Creation in Christ Jesus taken on the cross through the resurrected Christ Jesus' blood. You are redeemed and healed fighting sickness and disease. You are not sick trying to get healed. You are healed fighting off sickness. Healing has already happened. Receive your healing just as you have received salvation through the forgiveness of sin. It is finished. You have been restored into the image and likeness of God which is without sin, condemnation, sickness and disease.

Jesus Christ legally and judicially restored you back to your legal family as a Child of God in the image and likeness of God. You have all the legal rights and privileges as a son or daughter of God. You are BLESSED. You have life abundantly. You have the mind of Christ and the Wisdom of God living in you.

34

Authority Day

"Fraud" Day 34

First published November 7, 2018 in the Fraud Series – The Repple Minute

Day 34 of the Fraud committed by Satan against man

Authority

Merriam-Webster defines fraud as follows: intentional perversion of truth in order to induce another to part with something of value or to surrender a legal right.

Adam surrendered man's legal right of Authority to Satan in the Garden of Eden.

You have no authority unless you are under authority. Authority always comes from above a higher authority. Authority is a top-down process. To have authority you must be under authority.

Authority is an official, legal, right to act. You have no authority to stop a driver speeding through your neighborhood. However, a police officer has the authority to stop the driver. He has been given the authority by the police chief and local government over him. The police officer is a man under authority. He has authority given to him by the powers of authority over him. He has somebody who backs up his authority. The only way to have authority is to be under authority.

"⁶ So Jesus went with them. He was not far from the house when the centurion sent friends to say to him: "Lord, don't trouble yourself, for I do not deserve to have you come under my roof. ⁷ That is why I did not even consider myself worthy to come to you. But say the word, and my servant will be healed. ⁸ For I myself am a **man under authority**, with soldiers under me. I tell this one, 'Go,' and he goes; and that one, 'Come,' and he comes. I say to my servant, 'Do this,' and he does it."

⁹ When Jesus heard this, he was amazed at him, and turning to the crowd following him, he said, "I tell you, I have not found such great faith even in Israel." ¹⁰ Then the men who had been sent returned to the house and found the servant well."
- *Luke 7:6-10*

As a believer and follower of the Lord Jesus Christ washed totally clean of your sin, you have all the authority of the King of Heaven. You are in Christ and Christ is in you sitting at the right hand of God the Father.

You have authority over Satan.

You have authority over fear, anger, bitterness, lack, worry and injustice.

You have authority over sin and death.

You have authority over sickness and disease.

You have the official right to act with all authority in heaven with your position in Christ. Your authority has been given to you in Jesus Christ. You have been crucified with Christ and raised with HIM.

[18] Then Jesus came close to them and said, **"All the authority of the universe has been given to me. [19] Now go *in my authority* and make disciples of all nations, baptizing them in the name of the Father, the Son, and the Holy Spirit.**
- Matthew 28:18-19 TPT

Jesus Christ legally and judicially restored you back to your legal family as a Child of God in the image and likeness of God. You have all the legal rights and privileges as a son or daughter of God. You are BLESSED. You have life abundantly. You have the mind of Christ and the Wisdom of God living in you.

35

Promised Land

"Fraud" Day 35

First published November 8, 2018 in the Fraud Series – The Repple Minute

Day 35 of the Fraud committed by Satan against man

Promised Land

Merriam-Webster defines fraud as follows: intentional perversion of truth in order to induce another to part with something of value or to surrender a legal right.

Adam surrendered man's legal right of Authority and Destiny to Satan in the Garden of Eden.

Twelve spies entered into the Promised Land, yet only two came back with a **good report** and the other ten gave a **false, evil and bad report**. An entire generation of approximately 3 million Israelites died in the desert because they listened to the false report. One view is we **can** take the land; the other view, was filled with fear. We **can't take the land** we look like grasshoppers.

You are not a grasshopper. You are a child of God.

> "**30** Then Caleb silenced the people before Moses and said, "We should go up and take possession of the land, for **we can** certainly do it."
>
> **31** But the men who had gone up with him said, "**We can't** attack those people; they are stronger than we are." **32** And they spread among the Israelites a bad report about the land they had explored. They said, "The land we explored devours those living in it. All the people we saw there are of great size. **33** We saw the Nephilim there (the descendants of Anak come from the Nephilim). We seemed **like grasshoppers** in our own eyes, and we looked the same to them.""
> - *Numbers 13:30-35 NIV*

Here is how Caleb viewed God and the situation:

"**8** If the LORD is pleased with us, he will lead us into that land, a land flowing with milk and honey, and will give it to us. **9** Only do not rebel against the LORD. And do not be afraid of the people of the land, because we will swallow them up. Their protection is gone, but the LORD is with us. Do not be afraid of them."
-   *Numbers 14:8-9 NIV*

Caleb walked in the confidence of HIS Father God. You are a dearly AGAPE beloved child of God, there is no battle or fight that is too large for God. God has promised that HE will never leave you or forsake you.

"**26** Then the word of the LORD came to Jeremiah: **27** "I am the LORD, the God of all mankind. **Is anything too hard for me**?"
-   Jeremiah 32:26-27 NIV

15 For [the Spirit which] you have now received [is] not a spirit of slavery to put you once more in bondage to fear, but you have received the Spirit of adoption [the Spirit producing sonship] in [the bliss of] which we cry, Abba (Father)! Father!"
- *Romans 8:15 AMPC*

You are not a grasshopper you are a child of God. Know that your father loves you so much HE sent HIS ONLY Son to die for all of the world so you do not have to live in fear.

You can trust the promises of God.

You are more than a conqueror. Greater is HE who is in you than any problem or circumstance you are currently facing.

Jesus Christ legally and judicially restored you back to your legal family as a Child of God in the image and likeness of God. You have all the legal rights and privileges as a son or daughter of God. You are BLESSED. You have life abundantly. You have the mind of Christ and the Wisdom of God living in you.

36

Established in Righteousness

"Fraud" Day 36

First published November 9, 2018 in the Fraud Series – The Repple Minute

Day 36 of the Fraud committed by Satan against man

Established in Righteousness

Merriam-Webster defines fraud as follows: intentional perversion of truth in order to induce another to part with something of value or to surrender a legal right.

Adam surrendered man's legal right standing with God to Satan in the Garden of Eden.

> "You will be firmly established in righteousness: You will be far from [even the thought of] **oppression**, for **you will not fear**, and from **terror**, for it **will not come near you**."
> - *Isaiah 54:14 AMP*

Personalize the above scripture by putting in your <u>family name</u> or <u>your name</u>. Speak and say this out loud. Declare by speaking your righteousness for you and your family.

> <u>My family</u> I declare in the name of Jesus is established in righteousness.

> Even the thought of oppression or tyranny is far from <u>my family</u>.

> <u>My family</u> will not fear or be filled with terror.

> Terror will not come near <u>my family</u>.

Why and how are you firmly established in righteousness? Is it because of what you do or because of what Christ Jesus has done already?

You are established in righteousness because of the finished work of God's love for all mankind in Christ Jesus' death and resurrection. Jesus bore all mankind's sin so that we can become the righteousness of God in Christ Jesus. Jesus did this while we were still in sin so that HE could establish HIS RIGHTEOUSNESS in us. This is a free gift. We do not earn righteousness. We receive RIGHTEOUNESS just like we were born as sinners. We did not earn sin. We are sinners because of Adam and Eve. We are established in righteousness because of Jesus Christ.

I am established in righteousness because of God's AGAPE love for me by HIS sacrifice for the payment of my sin. HE took all sin, sickness, disease, death and the curse on the Cross by the shed blood of Jesus Christ.

All oppression, fear, condemnation, shame, guilt, inadequacies, lack and terror will be far from me. My provision and protection is established in my Righteousness in Christ Jesus.

And this will be his name:

'The LORD Is Our Righteousness.'
- *Jeremiah 23:6 NLT*

You are established in Righteousness through the sacrificial blood of Jesus Christ. You are established in Righteousness through HIS resurrection. All your sin past, present and future was nailed to the cross. The Judge of the Heavenly Courts declares you not guilty. The payment has been made in an Agape love offering by Christ Jesus. Christ has set you free.

You are established in Righteousness. God sees you as Holy and Righteous. HE has HIS Royal Robe of Righteousness for you to wear.

You are established in Righteousness.

Jesus Christ legally and judicially restored you back to your legal family as a Child of God in the image and likeness of God. You have all the legal rights and privileges as a son or daughter of God. You are BLESSED. You have life abundantly. You have the mind of Christ and the Wisdom of God living in you.

37

Calling

"Fraud" Day 37

First published November 12, 2018 in the Fraud Series – The Repple Minute

Day 37 of the Fraud committed by Satan against man

Calling

Merriam-Webster defines fraud as follows: intentional perversion of truth in order to induce another to part with something of value or to surrender a legal right.

Adam surrendered man's legal rights of abundance, health and life over to Satan in the Garden of Eden.

Paul tells his Testimony of seeing a light brighter than the sun and hearing the voice of Jesus on the road to Damascus before King Agrippa in defense of the accusations against him.

"¹⁵ "Then I asked, 'Who are you, Lord?'

'I am Jesus, whom you are persecuting,' the Lord replied. ¹⁶ 'Now get up and stand on your feet. I have appeared to you to appoint you as a servant and as a witness of what you have seen and will see of me. ¹⁷ I will rescue you from your own people and from the Gentiles. I am sending you to them ¹⁸ to open their eyes and turn them from darkness to light, and from the power of Satan to God, so that they may receive forgiveness of sins and a place among those who are sanctified by faith in me.'"
-   *Acts 26:15-18*

Paul's calling is the same as your calling.

Here is your calling _____ (put your name)

I am sending you _____ (your name) to

open their eyes

and turn them **from darkness to the light of God's love**, and

from the **power of Satan to God**,

so that

they may receive **forgiveness of sins** and

a place among those who are **sanctified by faith in me**.

- We are sent (called) to open the eyes of those we encounter to the truth of God's Spiritual eyes of love, forgiveness of sin, and righteousness (sanctification).

- We are sent (called) to turn them from the darkness of this world cursed system of painful toil and sweat which is the craving and lusts for provision, power, position and possessions.

- We are sent to turn them from the darkness of defeat, fear, selfishness, self-effort, jealousy, greed, unforgiveness, arrogance, pride, anger, bitterness, revenge, injustice, hopelessness, poverty, lack, sickness and death.

- Because the AGAPE love of the Father is in us, we called to point people to the (light). The "Light" is HIS AGAPE LOVE for all mankind when received brings eternal life and right standing with the Father.

The Light is the Father's redemption and restoration plan of growth, increase, abundant life, hope, joy, Agape love and peace in Christ Jesus (the Light). We can enter God's presence (Light) because of Jesus' death, burial and resurrection. There is no fear in God's (Light) of AGAPE LOVE

We are called to tell and proclaim that **Satan was defeated on the cross.** The Royal Procession has happened with the Resurrection of Christ. Like Goliath's head was cut off so Satan's Rule has ended. Satan was defeated by the Blood of Jesus Christ. God has given HIS CHILDREN power, authority and dominion to Rule and Reign to further HIS KINGDOM.

Jesus Christ legally and judicially restored you back to your legal family as a Child of God in the image and likeness of God. You have all the legal rights and privileges as a son or daughter of God. You are BLESSED. You have life abundantly. You have the mind of Christ and the Wisdom of God living in you.

38

I am a Child of God

"Fraud" Day 38

First published November 13, 2018 in the Fraud Series – The Repple Minute

Day 38 of the Fraud committed by Satan against man

I am a Child of God

Merriam-Webster defines fraud as follows: intentional perversion of truth in order to induce another to part with something of value or to surrender a legal right.

Adam surrendered man's legal right as a Child of God to Satan in the Garden of Eden.

I am no longer a slave to fear. I am a child of God.

I am no longer an orphan. I have a NEW FATHER. I am a child of God.

I am no longer a slave to sin. I am a Child of God.

I am no longer a slave to condemnation, shame and guilt. I am a Child of God.

I am no longer a slave to this world. I am a Child of God.

I am no longer a slave to anger, bitterness and rage. I am a Child of God.

I am no longer a slave to religion. I am Born Again with the Holy Spirit living in me. I am a Child of God.

I am no longer a slave to hate. I have the Love of God living in me. I am a Child of God.

I am no longer a slave to the past. I have been set free from the bondage of the past. I am a Child of God.

I am no longer a slave to what others think about me. I know my FATHER LOVES ME. I am a Child of God.

I am no longer a slave to sickness and disease. I have been healed, restored, redeemed and made a NEW CREATION in CHRIST JESUS. I am a child of God.

I am no longer a slave to my mind. I have put on the Mind of Christ. I am a Child of God.

I am no longer a slave to man's thinking and reasoning. I have the Wisdom of God living in me. I am a Child of God.

I am no longer a slave to being offended. I am accepted and loved by my FATHER. I am a Child of God.

I am no longer a slave to being right. I have been made RIGHTEOUS by the Blood of Jesus. I am a Child of God.

I am no longer a slave to lack. I have the God's provision, prosperity and abundance overflowing in me. I am a Child of God.

I am no longer a slave to restless nights. I have entered the SABBATH REST in Christ Jesus knowing I am a Child of God.

Jesus Christ legally and judicially restored you back to your legal family as a Child of God in the image and likeness of God. You have all the legal rights and privileges as a son or daughter of God. You are BLESSED. You have life abundantly. You have the mind of Christ and the Wisdom of God living in you.

39

Declared Righteous

"Fraud" Day 39

First published November 14, 2018 in the Fraud Series – The Repple Minute

Day 39 of the Fraud committed by Satan against man

Declared Righteous

Merriam-Webster defines fraud as follows: intentional perversion of truth in order to induce another to part with something of value or to surrender a legal right.

Adam surrendered man's legal rights and became indebted to Satan in the Garden of Eden.

Why did God raise Jesus from the dead?

- "Who was delivered up because of our offenses, and was raised up because of our being <u>declared righteous</u>."
  - *Romans 4:25 YLT*

God is Judge in the Heavenly Courts, raised Jesus from the dead to pronounce and declare you righteous. It was a declaration of righteousness being pronounced to mankind. Here is the declaration:

"YOU HAVE BEEN MADE RIGHTEOUS THROUGH THE DEATH, BURIAL AND RESURRECTTION OF JESUS CHRIST."

The New International Version uses the word **Justification** instead of **declared righteous**.

> • "He was delivered over to death for our sins and was raised to life for our justification."
> - *Romans 4:25 NIV*

So what is justification?

Justification in Greek is "dikaiósis" which in the Strong's Concordance means the act of pronouncing righteous or acquittal. In Thayer's Lexicon, "dikaiosis" means the act of God declaring men free from guilt and acceptable to him; adjudging to be righteous.

You have been judicially approved and declared by God as righteous, not because of anything you have done but because of what God "did" in and through Jesus Christ on the cross. The resurrection is the judicial declaration that payment was made and paid in full for mankind's sin on the cross.

When a mortgage is paid off, there is a declaration of payment called a "Satisfaction of Mortgage." This legal document is a declaration to the public that this debt has been paid.

The Divine exchange of God's love was finished and nailed to the cross. Jesus took all your sins past, present and future and exchanged and imputed HIS RIGHTEOUSNESS to you.

Jesus' resurrection is the legal and public "declaration of righteousness" saying the "Divine exchange" is complete. Jesus' resurrection is the "Satisfaction of the sin debt" being paid and that you have been "Justified" - declared and judged righteous by God.

This should make you want to stand and do the wave!

You are the righteousness of God in Christ Jesus. The resurrection is your proof of payment through the judicial pronouncement and declaration of your righteousness in Christ Jesus.

Jesus Christ legally and judicially restored you back to your legal family as a Child of God in the image and likeness of God. You have all the legal rights and privileges as a son or daughter of God. You are BLESSED. You have life abundantly. You have the mind of Christ and the Wisdom of God living in you.

40

Believers Commissioned

"Fraud" Day 40

First published November 16, 2018 in the Fraud Series – The Repple Minute

Day 40 of the Fraud committed by Satan against man

Believers Commissioned

Below is your commission today as a believer found in Mark 16 [Amplified Version] with my comments (in parentheses) and Jesus speaking in **bold**.

"¹⁴ Later, Jesus appeared to the eleven [disciples] themselves as they were reclining *at the table*; and He called them to account for their unbelief and hardness of heart, because they had not believed those who had seen Him after He had risen [from death]. ¹⁵ And He said to them,

1. **"Go**

2. **into all the world**

3. **and preach** (Greek to proclaim, to herald, to publish, proclaim openly, something which has been done)

4. **the gospel** (*2 Corinthians 5:21* "He made Christ who knew no sin to [judicially] be sin on our behalf, so that in Him we would become the righteousness of God [that is, we would be made acceptable to Him and placed in a right relationship with Him by His gracious loving kindness]."

5. **to all creation.**

"**¹⁶He who has believed** [in Me] **and has been baptized will be saved** [from the penalty of God's wrath and judgment]; **but he who has not believed will be condemned.**

¹⁷These signs will accompany those who have believed:

- **in My name** (You have legal authority with a power of attorney, judicial right as a born-again believer, son of God to use the name of Jesus.)

- **they will cast out demons,**

- **they will speak in new tongues**; (Life and death is in the power of the tongue/mouth/words which can cast out demons in Jesus' Name.)

- ¹⁸ **they will pick up serpents**, (In Greek "pick up" can mean to take away the rule of Satan the Serpent in a believer's life. You are a New Creation Life. You have authority over Satan to take him away and throw him away with all the consequences of sin's effect of guilt, shame, condemnation, rejection, and inferiority because we have been made righteous by the Blood of Jesus Christ.)

- **and if they drink anything deadly, it will not hurt them**;

- **they will lay hands on the sick, and they will get well**."

"¹⁹ So then, when the Lord Jesus had spoken to them, He was taken up into heaven and sat down at the right hand of God. ²⁰ And they went out and preached everywhere, while the Lord was working with them and confirming the word by the signs that followed."

Jesus Christ legally and judicially restored you back to your legal family as a Child of God in the image and likeness of God. You have all the legal rights and privileges as a son or daughter of God. You are BLESSED. You have life abundantly. You have the mind of Christ and the Wisdom of God living in you.

Appendix

Who I am in Christ

I am a resurrected spirit in an unresurrected body.

I am an agent of Redemption.

As HE is, so am I in this world.

Greater is HE who is in me than he who is in the world.

I am redeemed from the curse.

I am redeemed from the sweat of the brow.

I am redeemed by the blood of Jesus.

I am born of God.

I have the divine nature of God living in me, the breath of life.

I am God's hands and mouth in Christ Jesus.

I am in the resurrected Christ so death is behind me.

"I am God's workmanship created in Christ Jesus." *Ephesians 2:8 10*

I am a dearly Agape loved child of God.

I am alive in Christ and will never die.

I am a tree planted by the river and everything I do will prosper because no weapon formed against me can prevail. My roots go deep. I am planted by God. He gave me life.

I am crucified with Christ and I no longer live but Christ lives in me.

I am delivered from the evil of this world for it is the will of God.

I am the body of Christ and Satan has no power over me.

I am a child of the Father who adopted me and loves me.

I am an Heir of God and co heir with Jesus Christ.

I am in a new bloodline there is no generational curse; all blessings are in my new blood line.

"I am a fountain of Life because of the Righteousness of Christ in me. My mouth speaks life." *Proverbs 10:11*

I am a good tree. I bear the fruit of righteousness. I bear the fruit of the Spirit in Christ Jesus.

I am not limited by the natural because the supernatural Christ lives in me.

I am the TREE of Life grace, not the tree of good and evil law.

"I am a tree of life. My mouth brings life to others. I speak life into others." *Proverbs 15:4*

"I am a wise son. I harvest in the summer." *Proverbs 10:5*

I am a spring, a river flowing with living water out of which flows life giving words of healing affirmation, hope, love, forgiveness, and healing.

I am Righteous by the blood of Jesus Christ.

I am the Donkey that carries the King.

I am seated at the right hand of God in Christ Jesus.

I am free. What Christ has set free is free indeed.

I am a new creation in Christ Jesus.

I am no longer a slave to this world.

I am a King.

I am a priest.

I am redeemed brought back to my original value. I am of God and have overcome him (Satan).

"For greater is HE who is in me than he who is in the world." *1 John 4:4*

I am a New creature with the Life of God living in me.

I am the disciple Jesus loves.

I am a masterpiece.

I am fearfully and wonderfully made.

I am beautiful, vibrant and young.

I am salt.

I am accepted by God. Man can reject me but God has totally accepted me. There is no spirit of rejection in me. I am royalty. I wear the robe of righteousness and have the signet ring.

I am talented.

I am anointed.

I am Blessed.

I am strong, healthy and improving.

"I am a love letter from God. The word of God lives in me." *2 Corinthians 3:3*

I am full of Wisdom.

I am smart. I am a good learner.

I am gifted speaker.

I am who God says I am.

I am not who people say I am, I am who God says I am.

I am not the tail, I am the head.

I am not a borrower, I am a lender.

I am not cursed, I am Blessed.

I am approved accepted a masterpiece stamped by God.

I am qualified.

I am equipped with the ability of God living in me.

I am empowered.

I am strong, equipped, confident in God.

I am Blessed because all my sins have been paid by Jesus Christ.

As Jesus is, so am I in this world.

I am favored.

I am crowned with Honor and Glory.

I am seated in Christ on God's right hand.

I am the son of the Most High King.

I have been given God's loving kindness and tender mercies.

I have been crucified with Christ and I no longer live but Christ in me.

I already have everything I need.

God lives in me.

I am the righteousness of God in Jesus Christ.

I am an Ambassador.

I am who I am by the grace of God.

I am confident and can boldly enter into His presence because of Jesus Christ.

I am in Christ a new creation.

I Stand on solid ground trusting the Word of God.

I am attached to the vine.

I am a **New Creation** in Christ Jesus.

The **Old** I am is gone.

I am **Justified** made righteous by the Blood of Jesus Christ.

"I am **Sanctified**." *Hebrew 10:10*

"I am **Perfected** forever." *Hebrew 10:14*

I am and have been **Made Holy** once and for all in Christ Jesus.

I am, **As HE is**, so am I in this world.

I am **Redeemed** from the curse of sin and death.

I am **Reconciled** to God through Jesus Christ.

I am **Forgiven** for all past, present and future sin.

I am a **Child** of God.

I am **Righteous** because of what Jesus Christ did not anything I do.

I am **Healed**.

I am attractive.

I am organized.

I am **Restored** into my original God intended position and purpose.

I am the **Spirit** of love, power of God's ability and sound mind living in me through the Holy Spirit.

I have the Spirit of God who lives in me. I am a Friend of God.

I am a Saint, Accepted, Approved, a Priest, a King, am Holy, am Made to last, Will not fall, am Complete, am Not ashamed, am Clothed in righteous, am Productive, am Alive, am More than a conquer, am dearly loved, am Eternal and will live forever.

"I am the Light of life" *John 8:12*

"I am a Son of light." *1 Thessalonians 5:4-8*

I am a Royal priesthood.

My Heart has been circumcised.

"I am Free. It was for freedom that Christ set us free." *Galatians 5:1*

Kingdom of God
Light - Knowledge

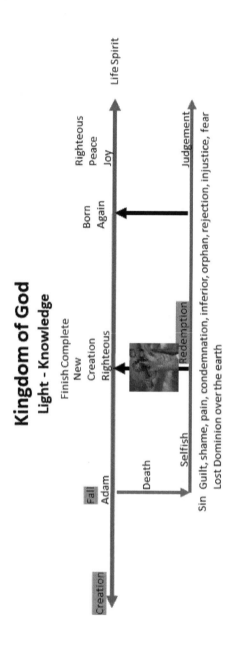

Creation

Fall
Adam

Death

Selfish

Righteous

Redemption

Finish Complete
New
Creation
Righteous

Born
Again

Righteous
Peace
Joy

Judgement

Life Spirit

Sin Guilt, shame, pain, condemnation, inferior, orphan, rejection, injustice, fear
Lost Dominion over the earth

Satan Prince of this World
Darkness - Ignorance

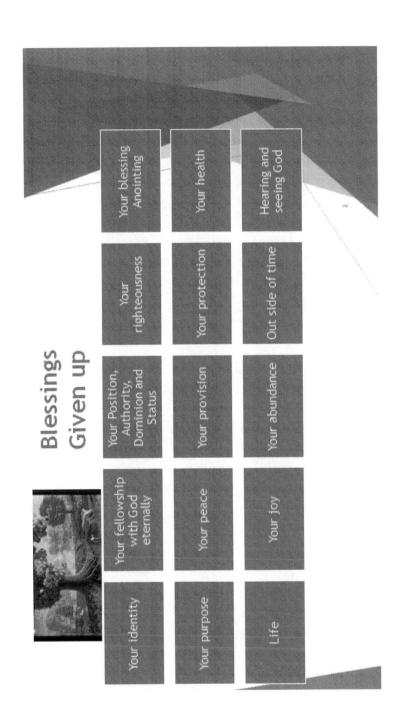

Blessings Given up

Your identity	Your fellowship with God eternally	Your Position, Authority, Dominion and Status	Your righteousness	Your blessing Anointing
Your purpose	Your peace	Your provision	Your protection	Your health
Life	Your joy	Your abundance	Out side of time	Hearing and seeing God

169

Exchanged For Curses

Death	Spirit of Offense	Regret	Injustice	Anger bitterness
Selfishness	Fear, worry, anxiety	Sickness and Disease	Shame, guilt, condemnation	Unforgiveness
Orphan Spirit	Satan Prince of this world	Scarcity	Blame	Poverty

About Glenn

Glenn Repple is Founder and President of the G.A. Repple Financial Group which manages several businesses including G.A. Repple and Company, a national broker dealer and securities firm.

Glenn's journey of preparation in the Financial Services industry started in 1972, and eventually led him to become a Regional Vice President with E.F. Hutton Financial Services. His responsibilities were to recruit and train Attorneys, CPA's, Insurance Agents and Stock Brokers to work together providing financial planning services to clients and businesses owners.

After 10 years of corporate training and experience and with an expanded passion for serving people, Glenn left E.F. Hutton in 1982 to become and independent Financial Planner to start G.A. Repple and Company. Since its founding, G.A. Repple has expanded with offices throughout the United States and licensed in 49 States. G.A. Repple has assisted in the formation of over hundreds of foundations and has raised millions of dollars to fund Kingdom of God purposes through tax and estate planning strategies.

Glenn is a CERTIFIED FINANCIAL PLANNER™, Certified Life Underwriter® and Enrolled Agent with the Internal Revenue Service. Glenn is also a Certified Biblical Entrepreneurship Teacher and Ordained Minister to the market place. Biblical Entrepreneurship is a comprehensive, transformational, business discipleship course that provides a strong mix of core business concepts and biblical principles. Glenn has trained over 500 business leaders who have likewise, claim, spreading the teaching into over 24 nations helping to fulfill Glenn's mission — "Helping people fulfill God's plan for their lives through business."

Glenn is also the past Board Chairman and Board Member of Nehemiah Project International Ministries. He is currently the Area Developer bringing the transformational Biblical Entrepreneurship training to Businesses, Business leaders, Churches, Boards and Ministries. Over 10,000 business leaders have been trained through Biblical Entrepreneurship. Most of the graduates of the program operate small to med-size businesses.

About The Repple Minute

A Free Fresh Start each weekday morning.

The
REPPLE MINUTE

www.TheReppleMinute.com

"The Repple Minute" is the daily morning minute designed to inspire, encourage, uplift and challenge your walk with the Lord. One of the major purposes of the Morning Minute is for people to know their Identity in Christ and their righteousness (right standing) with God in Christ Jesus.

Glenn Repple has continuously published "The Morning Minute" since 2006 to encourage, uplift and challenge us to step further into God's plan by recognizing the opportunities that are available through application of God's Word to our daily lives.

Enjoy the convenience of having "The Repple Minute" delivered directly to your email inbox - free of charge. Visit www.TheReppleMinute.com.

Contact The Repple Minute

Contact Info

Speaking engagements

Biblical Entrepreneur Teaching

The Repple Minute

101 Normandy Road – Casselberry FL 32707

Email | Hello@TheReppleMinute.com

Phone | (407) 339-9090

Online | www.TheReppleMinute.com

Facebook | Facebook.com/TheReppleMinute

G A Repple and Company
A Registered Broker/Dealer & Investment Advisor Member FINRA & SIPC